# THE NEW MAHARAJAHS

*Also by Claudia Cragg*

The New Taipans

# THE NEW MAHARAJAHS

## THE COMMERCIAL PRINCES OF INDIA, PAKISTAN AND BANGLADESH

### CLAUDIA CRAGG

CENTURY
BUSINESS

First published in the United Kingdom in 1996 by Century Ltd
Random House, 20 Vauxhall Bridge Road, London SW1V 2SA

Random House Australia (Pty) Limited
16 Dalmore Drive, Scoresby, Victoria 3179
Australia

Random House New Zealand Limited
18 Poland Road, Glenfield
Auckland 10, New Zealand

Random House South Africa (Pty) Limited
PO Box 2263, Rosebank 2121
South Africa

Random House UK Limited Reg. No. 954009

Papers used by Random House UK Limited are natural, recyclable products made from
wood grown in sustainable forests. The manufacturing processes conform to the
environmental regulations of the country of origin

ISBN 0 7126 7761 5

Typeset by SX Composing DTP, Rayleigh, Essex
Printed and bound in Great Britain by Mackays of Chatham, PLC, Chatham, Kent

Companies, institutions and other organizations wishing to make bulk purchases of
any business books published by Random House should contact their local bookstore
or Random House direct:
Special Sales Director
Random House, 20 Vauxhall Bridge Road, London SW1V 2SA

Tel. 0171 973 9000 Fax 0171 828 6681

This book is dedicated to the late Sir Henry Horsman, Bt.
to the late Wing Commander F.T. Cragg
and to all those associated with the Suadeshi Cotton Mills in Kanpur.

ACKNOWLEDGEMENTS
Among those who helped significantly with the project were a number of individuals at Barclays de Zoete Wedd, Cazenove, Credit Lyonnais, Crosby, CS First Boston, Goldman Sachs, Hoare Govett Asia/Smith Barney, Lehmans, Marlin, Morgan Stanley, Peregrine Securities, SBC Warburg, Schroders, Merrill Lynch (Smith New Court), and W I Carr. Also generous with their advice were The Hon. Nengcha Louvum, Commercial Attaché, Consulate General of India, NY and The Hon. Javaid Aslam, Commercial Counsellor, Consulate General of Pakistan, NY. In Washington, the Commercial Counsellor is the Hon. Mizanur Rahman. Claire Barnes was, as always, generous to a fault with ideas and Edward C. White, of Flemings gave me the great benefit of his considerable expertise. Ambar Paul was invaluable with his insight into those from the sub-continent now living in the diaspora. Professor Vijay Govendra Rajan at The Amos Tuck School of Business at Darmouth and Professor C. K. Prahalad at Ann Arbor, Michigan made helpful suggestions. Katie Cross and Diane Hart assisted most ably with extra research and the collection of worldwide resources for the project.

Of more general help in reaching a consensus on those who should be included were many dozens of highly informed and helpful respondents on the World Wide Web who encouraged and assisted in a flood of e-mail with the often obscure and otherwise hard-to-verify finer details. Many of these individuals came from regional universities via their sites on the Web and especially through INDOLink (http://www.genius.net/indolink/). Other web sources for corroboration of facts were:-
The Asia Business Connection (http://www.asia.biz.com)
The Asia Business Database (http://twnon-line.hinet.net/globald.eindex.htm)
Explore India http://www.explore.india.com/)
Gateway to India (http://www.bagade.com)
The Hindu online edition (http://www.webpage.com/hindu/)
The India Virtual Library (http://webhead.com/WWWVL/India/)

The India Home Page (http://mathiab.sunysb.ed/~cpandya/india.html/)
and India Online (http://indiaonline.com/).
Numerous and similar sources were used for Pakistan and Bangladesh.

I am indebted also to Patrick Walsh, Elizabeth Hennessy, Simon King, David Parrish, Jane Selley, Roger Walker, Marie Lorimer and to Kate Stone, Lisa Claffey, Linda Pulkowski, Suzie & Steve Boyett, and to Brendan Egan, Donna and Dick Strong, Shirish Malekar and Mary Beth and Dick Weiss. And also to Maud Dodson, Lucy & Professor Norman Morris, Dr. Roxanna Chapman, Mlle Boudier, SPGS, Sister Richard I.B.V.M. and to Adam, Tobias and Cleo. My greatest debt however is to Anthony L T Cragg who was as always a font of expert knowledge and inspiration on a subject that would otherwise have proved too daunting.

Note: figures expressed in dollars ($) refer to US dollars unless otherwise indicated.

# Contents

# Foreword

When foreign journalists in the early 1990s portrayed India as 'the next tiger', i.e. the next economy to enjoy a fierce rate of growth, its finance minister suggested that his country might not aspire to be such an aggressive animal, but instead cast itself as an elephant. Those familiar only with the elephant's lumbering gait thought this unambitious. Indians, who revere the elephant's gentleness and wisdom, also know that it is one of the few animals which a tiger cannot better, and respect its phenomenal strength and endurance.

It is now clear that the elephant and the tiger are pursuing slightly different courses, as befits their differing priorities, and that those who wish to prosper in the twenty-first century will be well-advised to learn the ways of both.

India already accounts for one sixth of the world's population, and for three of its fifteen largest cities. Now that it has discarded its inward-looking socialist policies, it is stepping forward to play its full role in the world economy – which means a tremendous expansion in trade and investment.

Makers of Western consumer goods salivate at the very visible spending power of the Indian super-rich, some of whom will be portrayed in this book, and at the statistics of the growing middle class, which, depending on definition, may be estimated at anywhere between 30 and 300 million. Administration, accounting and the rule of law look reassuringly familiar to newcomers; English is the common language of business; satellite television has facilitated brand advertising. However, many such companies soon discover that tapping the Indian market is no pushover, and that their local competitors need to be taken rather seriously. They discover a myriad of small cultural and practical singularities; they encounter an equal

1

number of minor obstacles and frustrations. In this difficult operating environment, great fortunes are being forged, but it is notable that most are being made by the locals.

The multinationals which do succeed are those which best understand local ways. Some become totally assimilated – Indians admire the formidable strengths and cash generation of Hindustan Lever; many think it *is* a local company. Others prosper with joint ventures, but in India even more than elsewhere it is vitally important to choose your partner well.

What, then, could be more useful and timely to the international businessman or investor wishing to participate in this great market than an introduction to his prospective competitors and partners, the new maharajahs?

Claire Barnes
(Author of *Asia's Investment Prophets: Top Money Managers and their Secrets of Success*, and managing director of an investment research company, Q.E.D., based in Bangalore, southern India.)

# Introduction:

# Mahouts in a Tiger Hunt

*Then he described a tiger hunt and the manner in which the mahout of his elephant had been pulled off his seat by one of the infuriate animals.*
W. M. Thackeray, *Vanity Fair*

Few areas of the world are more evocative than the Indian subcontinent, with its exotic natural beauty and extraordinary contrasts. Many business visitors, though, are daunted by the sheer size of the country, and by the multiplicity of cultures, languages and religions. Modern India is made up of twenty-five states, some of which are bigger than many independent countries, and seven union territories. Uttar Pradesh, with a population of almost 130 million people, twice that of Britain, would be the eighth biggest independent state in the world, though as the centre of the Hindi-speaking heartland it is not pressing for separation. West Bengal, with nearly 60 million people and a government that claims to be Marxist-Communist, is very different in temperament and political hue from its neighbour, Bihar. Further to the north and east are the Assamese, whose government has been paralysed by running battles with dissidents hostile to rule from Delhi.

All of this diversity is in the north of India, where there is a common Aryan inheritance. While the ancestors of the northern Indians came to the country from the west and north, the people in the south, the original inhabitants of the subcontinent, are Dravidians. Their skins on the whole are darker, and they speak languages unrelated to the north Indian tongues, which share a common ancestry with European language. The south has resisted the attempts of the north – starting with the great democrat Nehru himself – to impose Hindi as the country's national language, and would rather speak

3

English. However, even in the south there are differences and local assertions of desire for autonomy. The Telugu-speaking people of Andhra Pradesh, for instance, have demanded, so far unsuccessfully, that they be given their own state.

The Indian constitution enumerates sixteen official languages, but the number of different tongues and dialects spoken throughout the country actually runs to around a thousand. English should not be underestimated in importance, though, as the key means of communication in business.

Apart from Hinduism and the Muslim minority, India embraces a number of other religions. Although the great majority of the country's 900 million-plus people do call themselves Hindus, the figures show that there are more than 100 million Muslims, 25 million Christians, 20 million Sikhs (concentrated in Punjab state in the north-west), as well as Buddhists, Parsees, Jains, Jews and various tribal people, some of whom still follow animist practices. With such a number and diversity of minorities, the potential for disastrous conflict is greater than anywhere else in the world. Even the bloodbath at Independence in 1947 would pale into insignificance, simply because the population has more than doubled since then. The annual increase is around 17 million, or more than the total population of Australia each year.

The predominance of Hinduism is key as a form of social cohesion, a glue as well as a religion. Yet there are other, more subtle threads that hold this nation together. Almost as big as Europe, it is to most outsiders intimidating because of the frequent eruptions and secessionist warfare, widespread corruption, disease and natural disasters. The unwieldy public sector paralyses the country, with its hold on the infrastructure contributing to continual power shortages, and bureaucracy is an art form. Poverty is everywhere, and the country is strewn from end to end with the most unfortunate of beggars. India's neighbours, Pakistan and Bangladesh, partitioned for the last fifty years, are even worse off. The contrasts of extreme wealth and extreme poverty are evident throughout the subcontinent, in housing, transport, dress and health. In this nation, a population which is four times that of the United States is crammed into a space that constitutes just one third of US territory. Half the country's people are seriously poor, in a way that even the worst slums of the Bronx could never envisage.

Despite the appalling poverty prevalent on the subcontinent, there has arisen a new ruling commercial class, the new maharajahs, a disparate group of business people with varied origins. Whereas the maharajahs of old devoted much of their wealth to great building projects, the new maharajahs are constructing, as their prosperity increases and spreads, a new society. The former princes had their power curtailed in the early 1970s by Indira Gandhi's socialist-leaning government, which limited their lucrative property rights and officially nullified their royal status. The legacies that remain are their forts and palaces, which provide a valuable asset for tourism. In Rajasthan alone – an arid state in north-western India where wealthy maharajahs once erected sprawling fortresses and extravagant palaces – there are today more than fifty palace-hotels. They include the Meherangarh Fort, the fifteenth-century fortress that Rudyard Kipling described as the creation of 'angels, fairies and giants'. The Umaid Bhawan Palace in Jodhpur took some 3,000 workers sixteen years to build, and now incorporates both a palace and a hundred-room hotel. Jaisalmer, a remote desert city not far from the border with Pakistan, boasts a sprawling hilltop fortress with ninety-nine huge cone-shaped bastions. The golden-yellow sandstone stronghold is strikingly beautiful in spite of a gruesome history. In Udaipur, sometimes referred to as the Venice of the East, is the City Palace, which incorporates a museum and two hotels. One of the latter, the Shivniwas Palace, overlooks Lake Pichola and the white marble edifice of the Lake Palace hotel, which, because it covers the whole of a small island, appears to float. Its occupier, the Maharajah of Mewar, was not the first of his peers to go into the hotel trade, but he is unique in that he has expanded his business beyond his own palaces and manages seven of his eight hotels himself. He commands great respect in Udaipur, partly because of his ancestry, but also because of the extent to which he contributes to the local economy. His enterprises employ more than a thousand people and support many times that number. All maharajahs, old and new – and indeed all Indians – believe that respect is not automatic and has little to do with lineage. There is a general compulsion in society to conduct oneself in business in a way that would make ones descendants proud.

While most people are aware that India is one of the very poorest nations on earth, what is less well known is that it is said to have some 110 million wealthy inhabitants, amounting to an eighth of its massive population. The country is the world's fifth-largest economy based on purchasing-power parity, and is actively courting foreign investors. There are also enough people able to contribute to the national savings rate of around 22 per cent, with the result that funding for economic growth can be sustained without complete dependence on investment from overseas. Management personnel in India have advanced technical skills and professional qualifications. The country also has a large pool of educated people who understand a market economy, the importance of customer service, and the challenge of being a global competitor. Investors appreciate the fact that India's management personnel adapt well to foreign cultures and make good international managers. In addition, India offers foreign investors competitive labour costs and workers with the potential to meet high productivity and quality standards.

The death knell of nearly half a century of socialism that was the Nehru legacy was sounded in 1992 by the then prime minister Narasimha Rao of the Congress Party. Today, fifty years after Independence, India finds itself commercially reborn, even though a stubborn one third of the industrial economy seems resistant to the privatisation wave and is still in the hands of the government. Nevertheless, the country and its people are rediscovering with an enormous glee an inherent entrepreneurial zeal and native business wit. The many Bill Gateses, James Hansons and Alan Sugars among India's vast population are contributing to the Bombay Stock Exchange's current capitalisation of more than $150 billion. That is a real increase from $85 billion in 1992, with the knock-on effect that the price of a number of apartments in the city has reached the $2 million level, on a par with the most exclusive addresses in Tokyo, Geneva and New York. India's economy has been likened to an elephant: it may be slow-moving and cumbersome, hardly nimble on its feet, but once it charges there is no question of its awe-inspiring might. The mahouts – that is, the drivers or keepers – of this particular economic elephant in the great tiger hunt of commerce are the Birlas, Tatas, Thapars, Ambanis, Hindujas, and many other significant business people.

India's complexity is intensified by its unique caste system. Other countries have social or economic classes, and may have special groups of people who are regarded as outcasts by virtue of their origin or occupation. But no one can match the all-embracing thoroughness of the Indian system. There are four main castes: the Brahmins, or priests; the Kshatriyas, or warriors; the Vaisyas, or traders; and the Sudras, the lowly or menial caste. The new maharajahs tend to come from the third caste. Besides these there are the Untouchables, strictly outside the caste system, whom Mahatma Gandhi christened 'Harijans', or children of God, in an attempt to elevate their status. In practice the caste system is further complicated by multiple subdivisions, but it lives on in everyday life. The higher castes disdain lowly jobs and often maintain strict marriage bars, thus making economic organisation of the country impossibly complicated. In Bombay or Delhi, however, the Westernised society moves so smoothly that an outsider would not guess that caste is important. In reality, though, outsiders often miss the telltale signs and distinctions of the system. More importantly, the capital is not representative of the whole of India. Outside the big cities caste does matter, and groups may fight to the death for their entrenched privileges. In general the Harijans have benefited from special laws to protect and encourage them. The higher castes were able to take care of themselves and enjoy a disproportionate share of the jobs, especially in the government.

More than 80 per cent of the population of India lives in half a million villages, in most of which the caste system not only survives but flourishes. But even in rural India there are significant variations. In the Punjab and Haryana the full flower of the 'green revolution' can be seen, with good crops, small-scale industries, and workshops springing up beside the roadside offering services from tractor repair to electrical shops. The success of local farmers has given rise to consumer industries and has provided jobs for immigrants to these states, mainly from Bihar and Uttar Pradesh. Political violence has not been able to stifle economic progress.

It is strange then that the world seems to have such a poor image of India and its potential as a business destination. Investors jumped eagerly into countries like Mexico and mainland China, both of which have problems just as great as India's, with perhaps fewer strengths. In India, on the back of a period of stable democratic government, with total national foreign debt of around $95 billion (compared with, say, Mexico's at nearly ten times that), there has been a growth rate of 6 per cent. The prevailing opinion is that, like many emerging markets, India is only in a period of economic adolescence, but that is to ignore the fact that it is also a 5,000-year-old culture and the home to much of substance in the civilisations of the West. Despite apparent internal chaos, India has made it to tenth position in the league table of industrial production, and is stealing many other countries' thunder in specific sectors. The Japanese, German and other corporate investment in companies in cities like Bangalore, India's 'Silicon City', bear witness to the fact that there are those who do know that India has arrived in the modern world. The potential size of the country's market, its location, the availability of significant natural resources and its highly intelligent, skilled people make India an attractive priority for global business. These factors, along with its language and cultural and educational facilities, make it a competitor to China for foreign investment. Undoubtedly, India will increasingly become a more serious contender in the future.

Yet most opinions of India apparently continue to be formed on the basis of such indicators as the Forbes' list, or coverage in *Fortune* magazine. Forbes names only two billionaires from the subcontinent. Although this is in part due to the fact that the real value of wealth is not reflected by exchange rates, it is also because of the lack of hard information about, and exposure to, the large number of powerful people in India, Pakistan and Bangladesh. It is also true that until Narasimha Rao's programme of liberalisation, which saw a boom in Indian business, few outsiders took much interest in the country. With the fiftieth anniversary of the end of British rule in India, however, it is timely to take a fresh look at the country in a modern context.

The powers that be today are not the old Indian princes, maharajahs and nawabs. Although many of them are still around and often in gainful employment or business, they just do not have the power they used to enjoy, despite the fact that they include super-rich families like the Jaipurs and the Hyderabads. Whether kings or commoners are under discussion, however, all have the same habit of spreading their assets throughout their extended family and frequently around the world, so that tracking down real wealth is a mixture of detective work based on solid commercial information, interviews and even induction. Family-owned companies based in India have varied holdings and experience many of the same difficulties that face family businesses throughout Asia. In response they are keeping profitable or core businesses and selling those in markets that are too competitive. Key members of the families are developing their management skills: many have attended one or other of India's half-dozen good management schools, or have been educated in the West. Education now matters more than ever.

Until India began to open up its markets in 1991, more money could be made from winning licences, which were often monopolies protected by high tariff barriers, than from genuine trading. But India's dynasties, like those of China, are changing. The type of business a new maharajah enters is the key to his success. His choice must be based on a desire to be in one particular sector, and to make a lot of money by using his cash and connections to grab franchises in fast-growing businesses. In complete contrast to countries such as Britain and the United States, India is concentrating on turning entrepreneurs into professional managers.

Although the democratic process in India has always been convoluted in terms of voting patterns, stable government over the last few years has allowed the private sector to work hand in hand with hopelessly inefficient state enterprises, with the result that success in business is measured by real profits rather than by the numbers of people employed. The future looks a little more uncertain, and it could be that tomorrow's governments are less friendly to foreigners and to business, but as one distinguished expert put it, 'Life will probably continue as before – with a corrupt and indecisive government, and the only executive decisions being taken by the Supreme Court. All but the most unhedged single-bet business people should be able to cope.' Elections do not change the broad direction of the economy.

The political background to the rise of the new maharajahs is significant. In May 1991, when the country was already in dire economic and political straits, the dynasty that had ruled India virtually since Independence lost dominance when Rajiv Gandhi was killed by a bomb while campaigning in Tamil Nadu in south India. Gandhi's Congress (I) Party chose his Italian-born widow Sonia as his successor as party president, but she rejected their invitation. When the electoral process was resumed after a period of mourning, the Congress Party gained a sympathy vote, but not large enough to form a majority government. The Bharatiya Janata Party (BJP) came second, while the then prime minister, Chandra Shekhar, rated only a handful of supporters. After protracted political wranglings, Congress chose V. Narasimha Rao, a seventy-year-old southerner, as party leader and thus prime minister.

Gandhi's assassination was just another problem in a country beset, at the time, by so many. Money sent home by Indians working abroad, which had for several years propped up the ailing balance of payments, plummeted as thousands of workers had to be evacuated from the Middle East because of the Gulf War. By 1989 India's foreign debts had trebled in less than a decade; they now equalled one quarter of the country's GNP and were two and a half times the value of total exports. At that time, annual repayments were well over 30 per cent of export earnings, though were not yet as high as those in some Latin American countries.

At the time of Gandhi's death foreign debts had swollen to more than $70 billion, and India's reserve had dropped to just enough to pay for two weeks' imports. Securities were sold to meet interest payments, and the finance minister had to go cap in hand to Tokyo to seek help. To sweeten his journey, India removed from a blacklist five Japanese companies which had been accused of paying bribes in an effort to win a pipeline contract. The concession worked: Japan provided $300 million in emergency aid, but their credit rating agency also lowered Indian paper to BBB grade, meaning that institutions lending to India did so at their own risk. In spite of the country's evidently parlous economic plight, however, India's politicians refused to swallow the painful medicine of a budget. At Rajiv Gandhi's behest they postponed it until after the imminent election, and instead passed an interim budget, allowing the government to conduct business without the pain of the tax measures which the International Monetary Fund was demanding as essential for new loans.

On the political front, India was once again thrown into an election just as the finance minister was forced to travel to Japan to beg for money. In late 1989 the Indian electorate voted for an end to the Nehru dynasty that had ruled the country almost without interruption since Independence and clearly no longer trusted the Congress I Party of Rajiv Gandhi. It was for these elections that Gandhi had been campaigning. The Congress party was whittled down to only 192 seats in the 545-seat House of the People, the Lok Sabha. The party that formed the government, the Janata Dal, was led by Vishwanath Pratap Singh and was the second largest in parliament with 143 seats in an uneasy coalition. The support of two parties outside the government was crucial to the coalition. These were the Hindu Nationalist Bharatiya Janata Party and the Marxist-led Left Front. Singh was chosen as prime minister, fighting off some of his own supporters, notably Chandra Shekhar, and Devi Lal, a Jat farmer in his mid-seventies from Haryana. The anti-Singh campaign was supported by disgruntled millionaire industrialists unhappy with the future prime minister's crusade against corruption and by Congress mischief-makers.

At the time a notable magazine commented that the situation was a replay of Indian politics at its filthiest and grimiest – money, muscle, treachery, self-interest, blind ambition – playing havoc with the people's electoral verdict.

Singh comes from a royal family in the largest state in India, Uttar Pradesh, and had been in Rajiv Gandhi's government as finance minister. He was known to be just and a stickler for chasing some of the country's great corporate tax evaders. It was his subsequent very successful campaign against corruption that directly contributed to the increase in support for the BJP, especially in the northern Hindi-speaking heartland.

In only a short while, Singh fell foul on the question of the destruction of the Muslim mosque in the town of Ayodhya where Hindu nationalists wished to erect their own monument and on the question of preferment for the 'backward castes.' The hostility towards affirmative action was met with widespread demonstrations and some students immolated themselves in protest. Singh was seen as too inflammatory to remain in power with the result that his government fell in late 1990. Singh's former colleague defected and claimed to head the *real* Janata Dal party, 'Janata Dal (S)' where S means socialist. Singh resigned, leaving Chandra Shekhar, who had been one of the leading lights of Mrs Gandhi's Congress, to form a government as a minority leader. Singh made a powerful speech:

> Hinduism is above all a religion of synthesis. It has united the animate with the inanimate, the soul of one with the soul of all, the *atma* (heart) with the *parmatma* (God). Islam teaches brotherhood with equality. Christianity lit the lamp of compassion. Buddhism and Jainism brought the message of nonviolence. Sikhism opened its door to the people of all castes, religions and social state. Where in all this is the conflict? The conflict is elsewhere. And religion is only a pretext. Religion is a lamp of the soul. Let it light your way.

Chandra Shekhar formed a government with Devi Lal as deputy PM. Large numbers of his relatives were given jobs and other perks. The widow of Sanjay Gandhi, who had been killed in an air crash, now became minister of state for the environment. The World Bank was criticising India for its economic condition and the Gulf War saw

11

India taking a position in which it forbade military planes from the US permission for refuelling.

The heated political temperature continues. In the Punjab the Sikhs would like a separate state of Khalistan, a situation that had once caused Mrs Gandhi to send troops in to murder the Sikh leader Jarnal Singh Bhindranwale when he made demands for the Sikhs: she cracked down on Bhindranwale and blockaded him in the Golden Temple in Amritsar. To the north, problems persist in Kashmir. At the time of Independence, Kashmir had a Hindu ruler but a Muslim majority population. It was cut in two, with the valley and the capital Srinagar controlled by India, and the rest of the state, larger but less valuable, and including the territories of Gilgit and Hunza, going to Pakistan. This resulted in a war in 1965 and fighting across Kashmir in the Bangladesh war in 1971, but without any substantial change in territory. The leaders of the Bharatiya Janata Party have said that they plan to resettle Kashmir with a Hindu majority population.

Despite high intellectual and academic achievements by many Indians outside India, over half the people in India itself are illiterate. Large numbers of village people flock to the towns each year, some in hope, others out of desperation. Here life is more unequal than ever. The luxury hotels testify to a lifestyle enjoyed by increasing numbers of the growing middle class. The homeless on the streets show that it is a luxury that few Indians can afford. Today, the educated Indian middle class, used to television sets, fridges, motor scooters if not motor cars – probably numbers 100 million. Below the officially defined poverty line are those unable to afford the very basic necessities of life, about 380 million who have nothing at all except every possible incentive to change their situation.

When a full analysis of the years of British rule is undertaken, credit must be given to the fact that the British Raj in the two centuries until 1947 laid the foundations of a modern state, with a national government and civil services, armed forces, railways and communications. Indian families like the Tatas and Birlas built up considerable business empires able to make steel, motor cars and a wide variety of modern industrial products.

Indeed, shortly after Independence India was a bigger exporter and a bigger producer of motor cars than Japan. The first prime minister, Jawaharlal Nehru, Rajiv Gandhi's grandfather, was profoundly socialist yet determined to construct a modern industrial state. Adopting the Soviet model, he devoted large resources to building up the country's heavy industrial structure through a series of five-year plans. He managed to achieve a 3.5 per cent per annum growth rate, only just above the annual increase in population of about 3 per cent at the time. The problem was that at that time most of the new industries were in the hands of the state, bureaucratically controlled, overmanned, expensive and with few incentives to improve their technology or keep prices down.

Nehru also – naturally to his way of thinking – tried to control the entry of foreigners and their investment. He wanted nothing less than complete self-sufficiency. What Nehru in effect built was a 'licenced raj' where the rich used controls to become richer and to prevent new people coming into the market. At the same time the bureaucracy contained the key figures of control, those who dispensed their business favours where they saw fit or to those who would pay the highest price. No need was perceived to produce goods to meet the standards of the rest of the world, because in a climate of self-sufficiency outside markets were of no interest. Had India not been dependent for energy on imported oil and other raw materials they would probably have engaged in very little international trade at all. However the development of an efficient national irrigation programme means that India is today self-sufficient in food and effectively 'drought proof', and that the seeds of space and weapons technology were developed: in the 1970s the governor was able to explode an atomic device.

While the reforms of the last few years have not waved a magic wand to dispel these economic and political problems, they have caused a change in attitude and established the idea that there are opportunities for serious commercial success, both for the country as a whole and for individuals in business. It is true that, for the average citizen, progress is slow. Real economic growth averages only around the 6 per cent mark. With the population growing at around 1.9 per cent per annum, the complete picture shows an increase in per capita incomes of only about 4 per cent year on year. However, India now has hundreds of millions of people who can at least afford basic consumer goods, and a growing number who can buy household appliances and cars. Pakistan and Bangladesh are faring less well, but even in those countries there is a noticeable band of thriving businessmen. Mahatma Gandhi's words, 'We should go down to the poor and rise with them', now seem tinged with irony, for no one imagined that India would become so absorbed with the rising of the new rich and their recently discovered affluence that the voices of the poor would go unheard. Leading the way are the new maharajahs.

The reasons why those in business should take India very seriously are clear. In terms of sheer numbers − in other words just using the economic principle of the 'gravity model' − the potential of the Indian market is staggering. Current car production figures stand at just one car for every 3,600 Indians, or a total of quarter of a million produced year year. Even with its burgeoning population and relentless heat, the country still only produces some $2 million a year in sales of refrigerators for domestic use. In the service sector, India has until recently been dominated by state-owned banks. Now a mere handful of new private banks have been licensed, but there is room for ten times as many. Such figures are enticing bait for Western business leaders and manufacturers looking to move on from more jaded or saturated markets.

The new maharajahs, the key to the new business momentum, are thriving despite the lumbering and inefficient public sector and the snail's pace at which liberalisation is taking place. Even these impediments are not going to get in the way of inevitable and inexorable growth. The underground economy has contributed markedly to the expansion of the corporate sector, and has a significant part to play in the GDP of about $278 billion. But the main engine of growth has, as in the case of China, been business people in the diaspora.

Most importantly, a change has occurred in foreign investment, and now companies like Du Pont, Ford, General Motors, Corning Glass, Kellogg, Coca-Cola and Pepsi are benefiting from their Indian involvement. General Motors has done the biggest deal, a $300 million project to product cars in collaboration with Indian firms. General Electric and IBM are also involved with local groups. General Electric's medical equipment factory outside Bangalore is producing $25,000 ultrasound machines which are headed for France, Wipro GE Medical Systems' first export destination in Europe. Coca-Cola, along with a non-resident Indian company, is going to make fizzy drinks and snack foods for export, worth $100 million over five years. Some of the 200-odd proposals from overseas companies have been cleared within twenty-four hours by a bureaucracy that used to take months. Just three years ago the law in India was changed to allow greater ownership by foreign investors. Despite this, many companies opt for joint venture arrangements because break-even can be achieved more quickly (60 per cent get there within four years). Joint ventures also help in dealing with the numerous government organisations and regulations that still impede entry to the Indian economy.

These foreign companies apparently find the infrastructure workable, if in need of improvement, and enjoy the cheap, abundant and well-trained workforce: technical experts who would command a $100-an-hour salary in the US cost only between $10 and $15 in India. The accumulation of years of inefficiencies has been gradually whittled away. Regardless of changes in political power, it is a momentum that will be hard to reverse. Among recent reforms are the lowering of the corporate tax rate and the abolition of the distinction for tax purposes between widely held and closely held corporations. Corporate tax on Indian companies has come down to an effective rate of 46 per cent. The country is also opening its markets to foreign goods, with reductions in import duties on many items and a lowering of the peak duty rate from 120 to 50 per cent. The duty structure has been altered to reduce or remove differences between import duties on raw materials and components and those on finished products. India also plans to reduce basic customs duties on project imports and capital goods. These reductions, along with much greater freedom to convert the rupee into other currencies, now allow foreign companies to operate more easily in India's large and growing market. Investment, whether direct or into Indian equity portfolios, has been increasing and should continue to do so. There has been a rise in the activity of the Indian stock market and a surge in the foreign equity and debt offerings by various Indian companies. Direct investment is concentrated largely in power fuel, oil refineries, food processing, chemicals, electrical equipment and electronics. Working with the new maharajahs is causing optimism amongst foreign investors, many of whom plan to expand their current operations.

Although the new breed of Indian businessmen can be found throughout the subcontinent, the centres in which they seem to thrive best are Bangalore, Madras, Pune and New Delhi. Bombay is the best place for manufacturing and is particularly valued for its commercial infrastructure. Its coastal location also makes it a prime site for those wishing to be involved in international trade. The high-tech maharajahs flourish in Bangalore, with its strong educational facilities, well-motivated population, superior software suppliers and contractors, and developing industrial base. Its accessibility and the

15

availability of some government investment incentives also make it appealing. New Delhi is regarded as an excellent place for corporate liaison offices and Calcutta is one of the most investor-friendly administrations in the country.

The new maharajahs are making sure people realise that India is now 'open for business', and that it offers exciting potential matched only by China. Key business individuals are banding together to make sure that the country continues to address its economic and regulatory problems, and there is increasingly a real opportunity to build productive and profitable operations to offer competitive and high-quality products throughout the world. The race for positioning in India is on.

# Chapter 1

# The Big Players

A few short years ago, back in 1993, a huddle of high-flying businessmen could be found in a Bombay hotel, thrashing out all manner of miseries and complaints about the Indian government and commercial life in general. This group, who have come to be known as the Bombay Club, took it upon themselves to coerce the government into giving them, and industry in general, enormous tax breaks. They claimed not to be opposed to the then prime minister Rao's liberalisation, but rather wanted to curtail any negative impact on them personally should reform go too far.

The Bombay Club felt that if anyone was to be forced out of business it should be the lowest level of Indian companies – that is, the bottom 20–30 per cent – since, they argued, those companies could quite rightly be considered expendable. Their own commercial enterprises, however, the élite 15 per cent, must not be affected or an untenable situation would arise. The main aim of the group was, and still is, to stop attempts by foreign interests to take over their highly successful Indian companies. Given that the entire Bombay stock market was at one stage worth just $143 billion, only twice the market capitalisation of America's AT&T alone, the new maharajahs were afraid that they had become not only highly desirable but also eminently poachable. However, the Bombay Club need not have worried about foreign investors, for given the uncertain political climate, the real threat is from within. The external danger has in fact been dissipated, since now each foreign buyer may only acquire up to 5 per cent of the equity in any one company, with total foreign holdings limited to 25 per cent of the whole.

If – the very brave would say 'when' – India becomes a world economic power, it will be entirely due to one of its greatest assets, its millions of entrepreneurs. But it is the newcomers who are causing the biggest stir, and no one more so than Dhirajlal Hirachand Ambani, the founder of Reliance, one of the few Indian companies truly on the world stage. The born leader of the commercial brat pack and the prince of the new maharajahs, Ambani's story is that of all his fellow commercial travellers, with whom he shares so many ambitions and characteristics. Together with his two sons, Anil – a chemistry graduate and MBA from Wharton – and Mukesh – a chemical engineering graduate and Stanford MBA – he has built the family's $1 billion-plus fortune on the textile and petrochemical industries. Today the Ambanis are the most significant of the new maharajahs, largely due to the fact that they are the country's largest and probably most profitable entity in the private sector.

The group's main companies, Reliance Industries and Reliance Petrochemicals, account for approximately 10 per cent of the capitalisation of the Bombay stock market. The company is a casebook study in success: Reliance's textile division in Naroda, Gujarat, for example, employs 10,000 workers who daily churn out 250,000 square metres of fabrics, ranging from shirting to suiting, in one of the most technologically advanced textile mills in the world. Few machines are more than seven years old, whereas most of the country's other textile mills have equipment that is decades old and needs several times the number of workers to man it.

The single most important factor in Ambani's rise to success has been his distinct dislike of the traditional tariffs to protect the textile industry. He has concentrated instead on providing real competition for others. The son of a schoolteacher, he came originally from the tiny village of Chorwad, in the western state of Gujarat. At just sixteen he travelled by boat to Aden to work as a clerk in a French company, where he learned everything he could about trading and ended up as the marketing manager for Burmah Shell products. In 1958, he went home and started up an import-export business, trading in commodities – spices and fabric – between India and Aden. At the time there was a government requirement that foreign exchange from exports be used for the importation of other goods, so Ambani exported spices and brought in rayon. Later, once rayon was being manufactured in India, he exported rayon and imported nylon. The process continued with the export of nylon and the import of polyester, and a great deal of money was made, since the scarcity of the imports allowed Reliance to command high margins, often around

18

300 per cent and sometimes nearly twice that. If necessary, products were exported at a loss in order to obtain the money-spinning import licence. Wherever possible, Ambani saw restrictions as opportunities. This same approach to dealing with what could be seen as limitations led him to set up a distribution chain for his Vimal label of fabrics, a best-selling brand sold throughout the country in thousands of small shops. At the same time he has increased profit margins by producing at home those items his competitors could only buy abroad. One such example is polyester filament yarn for the production of polyester fabrics. In a deal with Du Pont that made Reliance their biggest customer for polyester technology, Ambani acquired the necessary equipment and set up in only eighteen months a 10,000-ton-per-annum plant on a 300-acre site at Patalganga, not far from Bombay. It is run by Ambani's son Mukesh, who has also set up a number of other plants for the manufacture of purified terephthalic acid and monoethylene glycol, both raw materials for polyester.

Ambani is sometimes accused by his critics of manipulating politicians, and of creative accounting. There are few businessmen in India who are not at least accused of these practices. Although Ambani was close to Indira Gandhi, and even closer to many of those around her, things have not always been so rosy. During Rajiv Gandhi's leadership the minister of railways, Madhav Rao Scindia, was a major investor in Reliance's principal competitor, the Bombay Dyeing & Manufacturing Co., a fact that may have led to the implementation of some policies unfavourable to Ambani. There have indeed been some incidents of note. In August 1989 the Bombay police arrested Kirti Ambani, a senior executive of Reliance, and accused him of being involved in an attempt to murder Nueli Wadla, the chairman of Bombay Dyeing & Manufacturing. The only 'evidence' was the fact that Mr Wadla had Ambani's business card in his pocket. Perhaps the affair was cooked up, as was suggested at the time, in order to abort Reliance's share issue, the largest the country had ever known. It is also possible that the government wished to present a tough image to a company sailing close to the legal wind. Ambani, like many others in the big business league of India, has on occasion been under some sort of investigation, at one point for the alleged diversion of bank loans made to family companies.

In the early days of Ambani's empire a great deal of time was spent hawking bales of yarn in Bombay's crowded wholesale market. He began the manufacturing arm of the company with only seventy workers and four machines, the best available. In those days, the family lived in a one-room 'chawl', a slum in a distinctly unfashionable area of the city, and Ambani's sons recall having to share their clothes. Ambani could not even afford an office, and so for two hours a day he rented a desk to serve as his business base. He is most proud of the fact that he has succeeded without the help of inherited wealth, education or family connections: 'I didn't have money and I didn't have family background,' he says. 'People often ask "Where did this upstart come from?"'

Ambani's skill at winning the ear of influential politicians has allowed him to monopolise the production of those products most in demand in India. He has been more than a little influential in persuading the government to cut taxes and import duties and thus boost Reliance business.

Those early beginnings have primed Ambani's philosophy that Reliance, and the family themselves, who own 30 per cent of the company, are, as he puts it, a sort of 'money pump', providing an opportunity for ordinary people to put their savings into a company that will contribute to the growth and prosperity of both the individual investor and India itself. As Ford did in the United States before him, Ambani declares that in India what is good for Reliance is good for the country. He is, it must be said, magical in his ability to get round India's wretched bureaucracy, and is a master manager in his field. As a result the family embraces almost four million shareholders, a quarter of the total investing population of India, which ranks third in numbers behind that of the United States and Japan. Ambani usually addresses his shareholders in a football stadium. The surge in investment from which the Ambanis have benefited is a nationwide trend. Things are very different from those days when the only opportunities for investment were with local government-run banks and the best fixed deposit rates on offer. These days profit is the by-word, and the government itself got in on the act a decade or so ago by setting up its first mutual fund, 'Mastershare', the net asset value of which nearly doubled in its first two years of existence.

The Ambanis have moved recently into the telecommunications sector, with a proposal for a $6.5 billion telecommunications project to provide a phone service in western India. The company is diversifying in a big way, with projects for the manufacture of television picture tubes and glass shells, while awaiting approval are applications for further schemes calling for $1 billion in investment. There are few challengers to Reliance on the horizon, either to take over the company itself or to build a modern-day commercial rival in any industry with equal clout. Anil, who is still only in his thirties, has thoroughly applied the benefits of Narasimha Rao's liberal policies to the growth of the company.

In recent times the Ambanis have been innovative in their winning of foreign capital for expansion. This was essential early on in order to fight off competition from those considered to be the 'old guard' of the textile industry. At one time corporate growth in India came exclusively from the acquisition of licences rather than from takeovers and acquisitions. In the early days Ambani fostered his textile operations by building up a small number of factories and creating a system of distribution to thwart the restrictions designed at that time to favour those in league with the government. As described earlier, the logical next step was to develop a capacity for polyester fibres for the mills, and accordingly Ambani eagerly ploughed money and effort into the petrochemicals side of his business. This was, as the *Economist* put it at the time, an almost 'breathtaking' exercise in vertical integration, which continues today with moves into oil and gas production for the manufacture of the petrochemicals. The Ambanis have always shown an almost Japanese willingness to invest in new technology, unlike many other Indian businessmen, who have traditionally preferred to rely on government protection to ensure continued business and profits. So while a number of companies are faltering, selling shoddy, overpriced items based on technology that is fast becoming obsolete, the Ambanis stay close to the leading edge.

The family also have ambitions in the engineering sector. The Larsen & Toubro operation, the biggest of India's construction and process engineering groups, has long been a focus for their takeover plans, since they already hold a large chunk of the stock. They want to establish further gas power plants and also plan to move into biotechnology and even electronics. It is said too that Ambani has a dream of becoming a Ted Turner or a Rupert Murdoch with the acquisition or creation of a daily business newspaper along the lines of a *Wall Street Journal* for the subcontinent.

Anil Ambani once commented, on the subject of Indian companies embarking on joint ventures with American businesses in an attempt at diversification: 'A lot of American companies are like taxis in their approach to doing business with us. That is, they start the meter when they award the licence and ask for a fixed sum in return, and that's the end of it.' That, he said, was not the kind of business the Ambanis were looking to engage in. The family are certainly not, however, adverse to diversification on their own terms. It was in 1988 that they made their takeover bid for Larsen & Toubro, at the time just one of a number of similar buyouts and attempted buyouts. In those days these efforts could not be anything but friendly, since in order to buy stock in a company, transactions had to be negotiated through the powerful government-run financial institutions, which in any case then owned just under half of the equity in all the major private corporations. It was this takeover and merger wave that saw a rearrangement of corporate power in India. Many of the old business families – pre-eminent among whom were the Birlas and the Tatas – have been pushed aside, and some have even disappeared from the scene altogether.

With the Larsen & Toubro acquisition, Ambani and his sons now control the third largest group of assets in India. In 1992, Reliance became the first Indian company to achieve Global Depository Receipts (GDRs) outside India, in this case in Luxembourg. GDRs are used to raise foreign capital, which is then re-invested in the company in such projects as new power plants and refineries. Many Indian companies, including the Birla-owned Grasim Industries, have since followed the Ambanis' example.

The family have pulled a number of publicity stunts, the most interesting of which involved an advertisement in a Bombay paper in 1988:

> Intelligent, educated boy seeks attractive alliance with girl of family with sound financial sense, who've invested in Reliance Petrochemicals debentures. No dowry. Family's financial wisdom main consideration.

In reality this was part of a $12 million campaign promoting a $365 million convertible issue for a Gujarat plastics project. The issue ended up being oversubscribed by two and a half times, with Indian investors piling in to the tune of almost $1 billion. Top of the Ambanis' list of priorities has always been to ensure that their name does not go unknown or forgotten anywhere in India, and the rich members of India's middle classes were delighted to jump on the family's bandwagon. It is interesting to note that the growth of the

Tata Group's company, Tata Iron & Steel, was eight times slower than the Ambani expansion.

The Ambanis have managed the bad times as adeptly as they have the good. In the mid-1980s, they faced a glut in the sectors in which they were producing, and had political problems at a very personal level involving differences of opinion and personality with the then finance minister V. P. Singh, who decided to straighten out what he saw as creativity in Reliance's business dealings. Profits suffered greatly during this time, but so did Mr Singh, who despite his efforts was unable to outlast the Ambanis. For the future, regardless of domestic politics – or rather in spite of them – Ambani is confident that there will be progress towards liberalisation in many areas, including imports. He also expects legal steps to be taken by the government to help resolve the issue of unlimited liability for foreign companies investing in India. As responsibility for the Bhopal tragedy continues to be thrashed out in the Indian courts, this remains a highly sensitive issue for potential investors. All in all the Ambanis remain committed, they say, to making India a part of the global economy.

Many of India's other movers and shakers are friends of Ambani, including Calcutta's Goenka family from the Marwari trading caste. Rama Prasad Goenka's grandfather and great-uncle were both awarded knighthoods by the British. Sometimes the very low-profile Goenka works in concert for takeovers with Manohar Chhabria, a man who shuns all publicity and gives out no information, but who recently took a business course at Harvard after becoming aware of the failings that his limited formal education might unwittingly lead him into. Then there is the young Vijay Mallya, who adores everything equine and is the proud owner of a number of prize fillies. When not at the race course he manages, at a very long distance, his brewery and liquor businesses incorporated in Bangalore. He may be a playboy but he works as hard as he plays, and his success is evident to all. He is based in London, and made one of the largest foreign acquisitions by an India businessman when he bought the Jensen & Nicholson Group, a British company that makes Berger paints. Then there are the Modis, who, when they are not attempting to defeat each other commercially have tied up the Indian photocopier market and are planning to bring out an Indian edition of the *Financial Times*. Last but not least is Ramesh Chauhan, whose Parle Exports owns two thirds of the Indian soft drink market, estimated at about

$400 million and with projected growth of about 20 per cent a year. For every one of these commercial dynamos there are dozens more up and coming at a rate equalled only by the overseas Chinese.

The positioning of the Ambanis and their commercial kith and kin with regard to the business dynasties such as the Birlas, Tatas, Oberois and Thapars is fascinating. These families are obviously not old maharajahs in terms of royalty, but neither are they new maharajahs, the modern-day commercial princes. Together they control about 15 per cent of the Bombay stock market's total capitalisation, and are very much of the old regime, that of the Raj, or more particularly the Licence Raj. This was the creation of Nehru shortly after Independence, and involved a restrictive network of controls enabling the rich to become richer and preventing new people and foreigners from coming into the market. While these dynasties are of course keeping up, very well in most cases, with the new business entrepreneurs, they are not cast in the same mould. The ownership of shares in most Indian companies has long been dominated by government-owned financial institutions, and until recently the grand families under discussion actually held only very small stakes, usually less than 10 per cent. However, when liberalisation began under Prime Minister Rao in 1992, preferential share allotments were introduced which allowed the great and glorious to buy tranches of shares at favourable prices. This was necessary it was argued, in order to fight off those all too eager to engage in hostile bids.

The vulnerability of these older companies lies in the sprawling nature of their business and in the way they were created out of the Licence Raj. In order to survive they are going to have to come to terms with change. As it was once expressed, competence not chromosomes or genes is going to win the day; that is, professional managers rather than family must dominate company policy. In most cases it does. The new maharajahs such as the Ambanis accept continuous change as an essential part of daily business, and indeed thrive on it.

Some time ago the Confederation of Indian Industry (CII) attempted a survey to decide which companies and sectors would best survive liberalisation. Their report was of more than a little interest to the new maharajahs, both as possible ammunition and, more importantly, as a revision tool for company policy. The CII's research showed that over the next few years the companies most likely to move from success to success are those involved in chemicals, leather goods, gems, jewellery, pharmaceuticals, software and textiles. Concerns arose over those in computer hardware and mechanical engineering products. The sectors that will achieve more gradual results are bicycles, motorcycles, heavy lorries and certain quarters of the chemicals industry. The new maharajahs need not worry that the state-owned sector of well over 230 firms will ever provide substantial competition. In total they account for less than 10 per cent of the GDP and have large unrecoverable losses.

For the moment, however, the dynasties survive. The Tata trading conglomerate was founded in 1968 by Jamsetji Tata and was subsequently expanded by his sons Sir Dorabji and Sir Ratan. In 1938, J. R. D. Tata assumed charge of the company at the age of thirty-four and continued at its head until 1991, when he was eighty-seven years old. It was then that the current head of the group, Ratan Tata, took over. Until the 1970s Tata's businesses were contained in two trusts which together owned approximately 80 per cent of the holding company, Tata Sons Ltd. In 1945, in view of the growth of the business, Tata Sons established a wholly owned subsidiary, Tata Industries Ltd., which became the group's think tank and vehicle for new ventures. The individual group businesses were run by senior managers with a common Tata approach, but in 1970, this system was abolished and the managers became the chief executives of the companies they were running. J. R. D. Tata's style of management throughout the 1970s and 1980s was to give complete independence to the individual CEOs, but when Ratan Tata became Chairman of Tata Industries this all changed. Ratan's biggest influence has been on group strategy, especially with regard to new ventures in areas such as high technology. Within the last five years, two company stalwarts – Darbari Seth and Russi Mody – have finally retired, making way for younger men.

Although it started life primarily as a trading house, the Tata conglomerate has been at the forefront of India's industrialisation since the start of the twentieth century. It threw itself wholeheartedly into both strategic and infrastructure sectors of the Indian economy when these were being set up for the first time, pioneering the hotel business in 1902, steel manufacture in 1907, electricity generation in 1910, oils and fats in 1917, chemicals in 1939, the automotive sector in 1945 and refrigeration and air conditioning in 1954. The group has also been a leader in encouraging and training staff for services in the national interest, such as India's first airline (now Air India) and the country's largest insurance company, New India Assurance Co. Ltd. These two companies were both taken over by the government as part of the nationalisation programme. Tata is also planning new ventures which are technology orientated and related to strategic sectors, and has entered into alliances with international leaders in areas like telecommunication services and equipment, airport technology and oil exploration.

One of the group companies, Tata Iron & Steel Co. Ltd. (TISCO), is the second largest of all Indian companies in terms of its total market capitalisation of $9.5 billion. Tata Engineering & Locomotive (TELCO) is third, and Tata Chemicals Ltd. sixth. The group also constitutes the largest Indian conglomerate in terms of turnover (approximately $55 billion annually), and includes four of the country's top twelve private sector companies, all leaders in their respective sectors. The Tatas also own India's largest hotel chain and the first privately held power generation company. Over 25 per cent of the group's turnover comes from steel, 22.6 per cent from commercial vehicles, 10.7 per cent from power, 8.8 per cent from cement production, 3.2 per cent from inorganic chemicals, 2.7 per cent from tea, 2.2 per cent from hotels, 2 per cent from software exports and 1.7 per cent from watches.

It has always been the Tata family philosophy that they have an important part to play in building India's industrial base. The family are genuinely altruistic and have engaged in a variety of activities which are clearly intended for a larger communal social benefit, as well as being good corporate common sense. Apart from their key role in Indian business, they have contributed in a significant way to areas such as public health (the Tata Cancer Hospital), research in the fields of science and the social services (the Tata Institute of Fundamental Research, the Indian Institute of Science and the Tata Institute of Social Sciences), and art and culture (the National Centre for the Performing Arts). The group also runs Tata Administrative Services, which trains professionals to take up management positions in their companies. They have always maintained a completely apolitical stance, which has allowed them to escape the turbulence suffered by many other companies.

The Tatas have always respected the professionalism of the individual managers of their companies – as well they might do, since they are known for hiring the very best experts in any field. When Ratan Tata took over as group chairman in 1991, he began to emphasise the group vision, instituting an overall strategy, with each company studied in relation to the whole so that new opportunities could be created internally. The Tata group has made three international issues of capital: TISCO's convertible bond issues of $100 million in February 1994; TELCO's GDR issue of $100 million in July 1994; and a GDR issue of $75 million by the three Tata Electric companies in February 1994.

Surprisingly, since they are not of the new generation of Indian entrepreneurs, the Tata clan also owns India's largest software export house, Tata Consultancy Services (TCS). Based in Nariman Point in downtown Bombay, the company is entering ever more high-tech areas and becoming more and more globally competitive. In 1978, the Indian government issued an edict which caused a number of American computer firms to shut down and leave, something which many in the industry in India feel has set them back years. The lack of competition is, they say, also the lack of a proper yardstick. At the time of the American withdrawal, according to TCS, companies such as theirs were working on a par with similar companies in Hong Kong and Singapore, and the government edict stunted their growth dramatically. TCS, however, does seem to have caught up, an achievement due in part to successful joint ventures with IBM, Unisys and Honeywell.

The name of the Birla family has been synonymous with Indian industry for more than one hundred years. The family is known for being low profile and philanthropic in outlook. The consolidated Birla family group is the largest industrial house in India, its 65-billion-rupee business empire made up of thirty-five companies spread throughout India and across five other countries: Malaysia (rubber, edible oils and chemicals); Thailand (mostly textiles); Indonesia (rayon and other textiles); the Philippines (textiles); and Egypt (carbon black). About one third of group turnover comes from the overseas companies. The Birlas have diversified their business interests into core sectors like viscose, aluminium, cement, textiles, fertilisers, carbon black and sponge iron, and they are the leader, or at least a dominant player, in every sector.

The Birla business philosophy has always been to achieve dominance in those industries they enter: that is, to establish a presence as a low-cost, high-quality and world-class player. The group companies are currently implementing major expansion and modernisation plans in order to further strengthen their position in the market.

There are several mammoth projects on the drawing board or at an advanced stage of conceptualisation, including ambitions to become more involved in the basic telecommunications service industry (in partnership with America's AT&T and in power generation (with Britain's Powergen). Birla also plan to set up a copper smelting unit (with technology from Outokumpu of Finland), and they are in the early stages of establishing a large bagasse-based paper plant.

This vast commercial empire is ruled over by seven different family factions which between them own and operate more than seventy manufacturing companies. It is the fourth- and fifth-generation descendants of the late Raja B. D. Birla, the founder of the group, who are currently running the business.

Until last year the late Aditya Vikram Birla, a chemical engineering graduate from MIT, headed the most significant of the Birla companies, which is twenty-fourth out of the top hundred Indian companies in terms of market capitalisation. The group will continue to be known by his name. Included in the corporate portfolio are such well-known entities as Grasim & Hindalco Industries, Century Textiles, Indian Rayon, Indo Gulf Fertilisers, Mangalore Refinery & Petrochemicals, Chambal Fertilisers, Birla Jute, Century Enka, Zuari Agro Ltd. and Hindustan Motors Ltd. Aditya's conglomerate, which is now in the capable hands of his son, is the largest and fastest growing among the seven subgroups of the Birla family. He had a number of other interests, such as membership of the advisory boards of two offshore mutual funds, and he was also the Honorary Consul General of the Republic of the Philippines in Bombay. The grooming of his successor began some time ago: Aditya's son, twenty-eight-year-old Kumar Mangalam, a chartered accountant and an MBA from the London Business School, was given full and independent charge of the most important of the businesses before his father's death, including Grasim's cement and chemical divisions.

Perhaps Aditya Birla had an easy route to prominence in the group because he inherited some of the most profitable of the businesses. He himself, however, made them grow several times, building them into large conglomerates by diversification into core sectors, all of which are in processing industries. Other group businesses are in textiles, and there has been a comparatively recent move into the financial sector. The Birlas have been quick to take advantage of situations where, because of the earlier system of awarding licences, two or more group companies find themselves competing with each other.

The competing companies co-operate with one another in terms of new technology, but market themselves fiercely, in order to egg the other on and keep them both on their toes.

There was always a clear-cut management demarcation between Aditya and his father, B. K. Birla, although they were said to enjoy prolonged but informal debates about aspects of day-to-day business. Decisions on all major issues – such as expansion, new issues of stock or diversification – are now taken solely by Kumar Mangalam. Since the businesses are technology-orientated, Aditya played a key role in conceiving and implementing projects and in operating the units. The Birlas have always followed the traditional Marari (the subcaste to which the clan belongs) control system known as 'partha'. This dictates that all operating profits must be strictly monitored on a daily basis, a task that used to done manually but is now highly computerised. The second line of business executives in the company is made up only of the very best the relevant industry can provide, and many of those in key positions have been with the family for dozens of years. The Birlas are well known for rewarding the tried and true with more autonomy in running their sectors of the business.

Grasim is just one of the late Aditya Birla's key companies which shows clearly the implementation of the Birla philosophy. It was set up in 1947 by Aditya's grandfather, G. D. Birla, as the Gwalior Rayon Silk Manufacturing (Weaving) Co. Ltd., and in 1954 was India's first producer of viscose filament yarn, better known as rayon. Grasim is now the world's largest manufacturer of rayon, accounting for 86 per cent of industry turnover in India, and the company has also diversified in order to meet its own needs for rayon-grade pulp and caustic soda. Other expansion has been into chemicals using by-products of caustic chlorine, and even into the necessary equipment. Grasim moved into cement manufacturing in the early 1980s, after the government's relaxation of the regulatory controls on the industry, and cement now accounts for nearly one fifth of the company's sales. Not yet satisfied with their multiplicity of products, they then moved into sponge iron, and in 1993 up and on into software and information technology services.

B. K. Birla's own group companies include Century Textiles, Century Enka, Kesoram Industries, Jay Shree Tea, Mangalam Cement, Bharat Commerce, Birla Century, Mangalam Timber, Rajshree Polyfils, and Manjushree Plantations. Century Textiles, which produce cotton textiles and yarn, viscose filament yarn, chemicals, cement, pulp and paper, and is involved in shipping, is the only one of the group companies so far to have accessed the capital market in a big way: in September 1994, for instance, they made a GDR issue which aggregated $100 million. Century, B. K.'s flagship company, is also his most diversified, and is the twelfth largest company in the Indian private corporate sector in terms of sales. It is the single largest exporter of cotton textiles from India and is a net foreign exchange earner.

Century came under the control of the B. K. Birla group in 1973, although it had been partially in their hands since 1951. The company started out in 1897 as a cotton textile mill, under the name the Century Spinning and Manufacturing Co. Ltd. The name was changed in 1987, and the facilities have been expanded and modernised from time to time. B. K.'s focus, not altogether unlike his son's, has always been the infrastructure and strategic sectors of the Indian economy. His pet theme has been the pursuit of corporate globalisation, and he is personally held in the highest possible regard throughout India and abroad, as an industrialist and a philanthropist.

There are a number of other companies sharing the Birla name. The K. K. Birla group owns four of the largest sugar companies in northern India and also has a presence in fertilisers, shipping, cotton textiles and cement, as well as running one of the leading newspapers in the north, the *Hindustan Times*. The C. K. Birla group owns an automobile company, Hindustan Motors, which has recently formed a joint venture with General Motors to produce Opel cars for the Indian market. The group's other businesses are paper, engineering, consumer items, cement products and jute, and it also operates paper and engineering companies in Nigeria. The M. P. Birla group has interests in jute, cement, and telephone and electric cables, and is the second largest manufacturer of cement in India. The Ashok Birla group has a presence in steel, special metals, edible oils, and industrial tools, while the S. K. Birla group is involved in fabrics, suitings, cement and engineering.

The Oberoi family is best known for its eponymous hotel group, which was started by Raibahadur M. S. Oberoi and which now owns and manages twenty-three hotels in six countries. East India Hotels (EIH) owns ten Oberoi hotels in India, while other group companies own another three. They also have four hotels in Saudi Arabia, two in Egypt and one each in Australia, Indonesia and Sri Lanka under the Oberoi and Trident names. The hotels are very highly regarded at home since they are one of the only three chains with a 5-star rating nationally, and are the second largest after the Tata's Taj chain. In the outside world they also have a reputation for high standards, with seven of the hotels, four of them in India, being members of the Leading Hotels of the World class.

Nowadays, the founder's son, sixty-six-year-old P. R. S. Oberoi, a graduate of the Institute of Hotel Management in Lausanne, is in overall charge of the entire business strategy and operations, assisted by his son, Vikram, and his nephew, Arjun. P. R. S. Oberoi's areas of specific control are strategic planning, senior management recruitment, pricing and interior design. Also deeply involved is seventy-one-year-old Gautam Khanna, the son-in-law of the founder, who looks after new projects and Mercury Travels. The second echelon of management is made up of industry professionals who have been well trained in reputable institutes in India and abroad. Some of them have been with the company for several years. There is considerable focus on human resources development, stemming from the vision of M. S. Oberoi, who set up the Oberoi School of Hotel Management for recruiting and training management personnel.

In terms of corporate standing in India, East India Hotels is twenty-second out of the top hundred companies based on total market capitalisation. Oberoi family members own 17 per cent of the equity of EIH, both directly and indirectly through Oberoi Hotels and Oberoi Properties, which hold 15 and 6 per cent respectively of EIH's equity. The hotel business has continued to be the primary interest of the group since it entered the industry in 1934. It is the company's stated aim to offer top-quality accommodation, although it is also planning expansion in both the upscale and medium-priced sectors through the Trident and Novotel (owned by Accor of France) brand names. One of the group's main policies is always to retain ownership of a property rather than managing one.

Although East India Hotels was formally created in 1949, the Oberois had entered the hotel business over ten years earlier, in 1938, when M. S. Oberoi took on the lease of the Grand Hotel (now the Oberoi Grand) in Calcutta. He later bought the property. In 1944 he took over Associated Hotels of India, at that time the country's largest hotel chain, and doing so availed himself of properties such as the Maidens in Delhi, the Cecil in Simla and others which are now in Pakistan. In 1952, Oberoi also took over hotels in Darjeeling and Gopalpur. By 1968, all the various Oberoi companies which owned hotels had merged with EIH, and in 1965, the family built Delhi's first deluxe hotel, in financial management collaboration with Intercontinental Hotels. This was followed in 1973 by the Oberoi Towers, Bombay, then known as the Oberoi Sheraton, and the Oberoi Bombay and Bhubaneshaw. In 1992, the Oberoi Bangalore was opened.

The group invests in new hotel structures rather than purchasing and renovating existing buildings. It believes in owning the hotels it manages so as to be able to maintain product quality and service at high levels. Graduates of the Oberoi School of Hotel Management are well represented in the company's senior as well as operating-level staff. The group's diversifications have been mainly connected with the hotel business, as well as with 'hospitality': flight and airport catering and travel-related services. These areas, however, form only a small proportion of the group's activity.

Another of the major 'old boys' in the Indian business network is the Thapar group, one of India's largest and most long-standing conglomerates who include in their portfolio the biggest paper manufacturer in the country. The Thapars also own a well-known brand name in textiles and are the country's largest producer of television picture tubes. In India that is an enormous number of televisions, with a still vaster market of viewers not yet tapped into. Thapar's prospects are looking extremely bright. The group has a variety of business interests, its main companies being: Ballarpur Industries, a paper, chemicals, food and agricultural products manufacturer; Crompton Greaves, producers of electric motors, transformers, switchgear and control equipment, as well as turnkey services; JCT Ltd., a textile, synthetic fibre and yarn producer; Greaves Ltd., makers of diesel engines, generating sets, gear boxes and general engineering and other industrial products; Andhra Pradesh Rayons, which makes rayon and paper-grade wood pulp; and finally JCT Electronics, manufacturers of television picture tubes. Thapar have key strategic alliances with global players like Westinghouse Electric Corporation, Hitachi, Mitsubishi, OKI Electric, Zimmer, Du Pont, Ownes, A. P. Mollar and Stora.

Each group company works on an individual corporate basis, concentrating on consolidating and growing its single and related lines of business. It is interesting to note the way in which the family cleverly avoided the problem of succession that some Indian corporate dynasties have had. The group's founder, Lala Karam Chand Thapar, divided his business between his three sons, B. M., L. M. and M. M., who in their turn have passed various companies on to their own sons and nephews. Family members influence group strategy and overall group direction, although the day-to-day running of companies is overseen by experienced professional managers. The family influence in the running of Crompton Greaves and Greaves Ltd. is less significant, however, since significant equity stakes held by multinationals mean that outside managers have more say on strategy.

After starting out in the coal business – a big cash producer – the Thapars moved quickly into several new lines of business. Ballarpur Industries, one of the oldest paper manufacturers in India, has diversified sensibly into businesses like chemicals and food. As a rule, however, the Thapars strive to keep or attain market leadership, and are spinning off any peripheral activities to concentrate their energies. They have been clever over the last decade in forging relationships which allow them to upgrade their technological expertise, while their strong political connections have been invaluable in the acquisition of revenue-generating licences.

The most colourful but difficult to evaluate of the new maharajahs are the Hindujas. It was the late Parmanand Hinduja, a devout Hindu from a village in Sind in the south of what is now Pakistan, who planted the seeds of the now vast empire, which today employs more than 25,000 people worldwide. He started out as a money-lender in Bombay, and then moved on to trading in tea and dried fruit with Iran, where he lived from the early 1920s, developing iron-clad ties with the family of the late Shah.

His four sons, still non-resident Indians, are family mastermind Srichand, and Gopichand, who are both based at New Zealand House in London; Prakash, who lives in Geneva; and Ashok; who has a luxury beachside home at Juhu Beach, Bombay. Ashok concentrates on the business of dubbing Hindi movies into Persian and exporting them to Iran. The Hindujas originally got into the movie business through money-lending, and continue to finance a great many of Bombay's present generation of film-makers. Their father left them some $4 million – land worth $3 million in Ahwaz, Iran, plus $1 million in cash – which, already worth a great deal at the time, has burgeoned massively to afford them a collective wealth today said to be well over $2 billion, though most of this derives from their 100 per cent ownership of the Hinduja group. Since it is highly unlikely that anyone could track down all their interests worldwide, however, this figure may well be an underestimate. They discuss business only in encrypted missives by fax or e-mail, and take long walks in parks to stop anyone from overhearing the content of their conversations. Such is Srichand's keenness for privacy that he dislikes giving a return address to correspondents, labelling the envelope for return only with the enigmatic 'Camp London'. The Hindujas' hundred-plus companies are said to be registered in the most unaccountable of places, such as the Bahamas, Liberia, Panama, Liechtenstein and Luxembourg. Among the best known of their offshore companies are the Geneva-based Alcara S.A. and the Panama-registered Metalco. Although the brothers' actual wealth is impossible to judge, their spending has long been of stellar proportions, and when Srichand's daughter Shanu was married in Bombay, many declared they had never seen parties quite like it.

There is a classical Parsi saying that advises that if you create enough of a mystery about the real content of your life and businesses, you will enjoy both power and prosperity for ever. This is something the Hindujas seem to have taken very much to heart. They belong to the traditionally secretive Sindhi community, whose policy is to trust only fellow Sindhis, and then sparingly. The turning point on the family's road to success came, it is said, when Indira Gandhi argued with the Shah of Iran over the high cost of Iranian oil. The Shah responded that India should increase its exports to Iran to cover costs, and with their Iranian connections, the Hindujas were supremely positioned to take advantage of the trade. One of their single biggest deals ever was an iron ore project, Kudremukh, for which they are thought to have received in excess of $10 million in commission. It is also rumoured that other Hinduja companies, Sangam Trading (named after one of their most successful movies) and Ashok Trading, acted as intermediaries in Iran for, amongst others, a well-known German car manufacturer, an American aircraft company, various computer businesses, a Japanese airline and trading company, and an American airline.

The basis of the Hindujas' trade nowadays is most significantly their holding in Ashok Leyland, an Indian bus manufacturer, which they acquired by fighting off competition from scooter manufacturer Rajul Bajaj (see p.42). In partnership with a Fiat subsidiary, Iveco, they bought into the highly prized Indian truck manufacturing subsidiary of British Leyland, acquiring a 39.9 per cent controlling stake.

It is apparently their intention to diversify from buses and lorries into tractors, three-wheeled vehicles and auto components, probably by taking advantage of a Japanese joint venture. The brothers also own the AMAS Bank, based in Geneva, and Gulf Oil International, manufacturers of lubricants, and are involved in a myriad of other businesses in every sector, including chemicals, fertilisers, ores, pharmaceuticals and steel. Their stated aim is to increase their ownership in Indian companies from its present level of around 5 per cent to some 30 per cent, but this has exposed them to the suspicion accorded all non-resident Indians who are perceived as trying to jump on the commercial bandwagon in the wake of the Rao liberalisation. The company has a number of tenders out for power and airport projects and for investment in the banking, media, telecommunications and television sectors.

The Hindujas at one point became involved with fellow new maharajahs the Tatas, who invited the brothers to invest in their London, New York and Washington hotels to the tune of $17 million, in return for a seat on the board. The liaison, however, did not last long, and the Tatas bought out the Hinduja interest for about $7 million more than they had paid for it.

One of the Hindujas' greatest strengths is their chameleon-like loyalty, which has allowed them to switch from a great friendship with the Shah's regime to alliances with Khomeini and now the present-day ayatollahs. Khodadad Farmanfarmian, former governor of the Central Bank of Iran, now serves as the brothers' chief financial adviser in London. And all of this despite the fact that the Hindujas made a quick getaway to London in order to avoid the trouble when the Shah fell. It is not just in Iran either that the family has friends in such very high places. When they give parties in London, guests may share the event with any number of world-class dignitaries, including former prime ministers Edward Heath and Margaret Thatcher, and the brothers were also very well in with US presidents Ronald Reagan and George Bush. Their companies are liberally sprinkled with those who have held high government or municipal office before joining the Hindujas to put their connections to the best possible use. One key company adviser is New York lawyer and former Kennedy associate Theodore Sorensen, while ex-CIA director Richard Helms provides another influential connection.

The Hindujas inevitably have established a mixed reputation. Some say that they are just middlemen in multi-billion-dollar arms deals and that they use their companies as a clever front. Many people believe that the family is engaged in other skulduggery and no-good wheeler-dealing of the worst sort – bribery, money-laundering and narcotics – although their many friends claim that such commercial pimping plays no part in the brothers' game. Whether to provide a smokescreen or not, the Hindujas regularly give away millions to charity. Financing for all Hinduja enterprises passes through either IndusInd Enterprises & Finance or IndusInd Bank, companies which have become savings vehicles for like-minded non-resident Indians who admire the Hindujas and wish to share in their philosophies, both Vedic and commercial.

# India

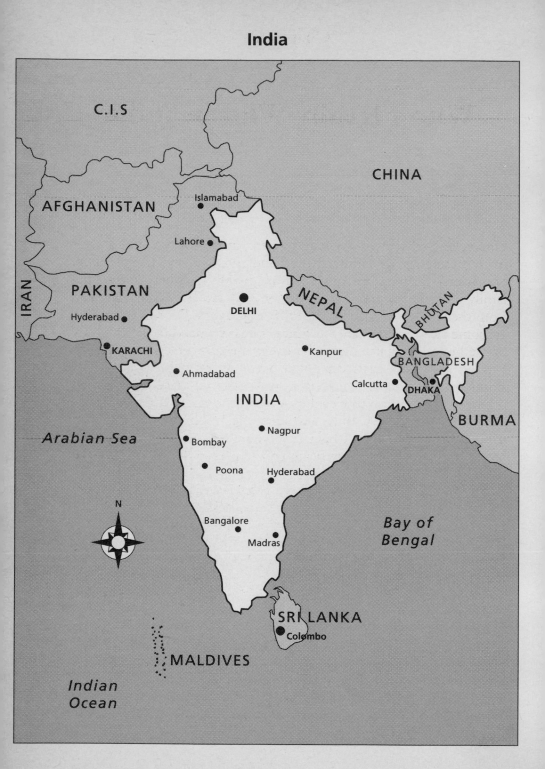

# Chapter 2

# Who's Really Who in India

Unravelling who owns what, and where, in a country where a great many businesses are family-owned and run is always troublesome. Sometimes fortunes are hidden from greedy members within the family itself, but more often than not cash and assets are concealed from the taxman and his bureaucratic colleagues. Despite this, there are some clearly identifiable fortunes, whose owners are as rich as any of the better-known multi-millionaires on the world stage. Certain families and individuals cannot be covered: the Raheja family of Bombay, for example, who have a real-estate portfolio among their other interests, refuse to be interviewed or to disclose any information about themselves. India also has a black economy which contributes markedly to the 10 per cent annum growth of the corporate sector, and which has a significant part to play in the country's GDP of about $278 billion.

The annual Forbes' list serves as a yardstick to give some measure of the world economic standing of individuals from countries that may be unfamiliar. This does not, however, take into account the disparity in true worth caused by a big difference in spending power. For example, in terms of purchasing parity, goods that may be bought for $5 in the United States cost approximately $1 in India. Yet Forbes' may only include in its ranks those people whose assets make them US dollar billionaires in terms of strict currency conversion, and thus only two billionaires from India who are also covered in this book – the Bajaj family and the Ruia brothers – are listed. This book hopes to shed light on those individuals whose interests may not yet warrant Forbes' attention, but who are nevertheless good candidates to make it on to the list in the near future.

Working as they do with quasi-British laws, complicated but fair elections, factory wages of only a little over $100 a month and a booming middle class, the new maharajahs have little in the way of business impediments to trouble them. Conditions for a successful future seem for the moment set fair. In this chapter a price is put on the total riches of those mentioned, but it is worth noting that the figure given is only an estimate of corporate – not personal – wealth, based merely on the value of publicly listed companies. When a family grows, its business leader will often hive off divisions of a company, or start fresh ventures under a new company. This is a practical solution to the problem of providing an inheritance for each new child. There usually remains, however, at least a modicum of connection between the resulting companies. Other assets are harder to track down and quantify. Though the sums quoted here will vary with the fluctuations of the rupee–dollar exchange rate, the reader may assume that these individuals are both wealthy and powerful in international terms. Even the obstacles of an inefficient public sector and slow economic reform cannot get in the way of their inevitable and inexorable growth. (Note: the Ambanis, Birlas, Tatas, Oberois and Thapars who would otherwise be in this listing are included in greater detail in Chapter 2.)

**Ashok H. Advani, Hiroo H. Advani** and **Rajkumar H. Advani** are the family behind the Business India Group publishing house. Formerly a practising barrister at the Bombay bar, Ashok, who graduated from Oxford University, is also a member of London's Middle Temple. Hiroo, also a member of the Middle Temple, is a Cambridge graduate. The brothers came to the attention of the business community as publishers of India's fastest-growing English-language magazine, *Business India*. Now there is diversification into Indian languages, and into video and audio entertainment.

*Main Companies*
Business India Database Pvt Ltd.
Business India Group
Business India Information Technology Ltd.
Operation Research (India) Ltd.

**Anil Agarwal**
Agarwal is the CEO of the largest private sector manufacturer of telecommunications cables in the country, and he set up the first private sector copper smelter in the country. He comes from a family of

metal traders and, much like many a successful East Ender working in the City of London, is considered by his peers to have 'made good'.

*Main Company*
Sterlite Industries

**Deep C. Anand** is a self made millionaire who has built up over the last thirty years operations manufacturing air filters, aviation and marine filters, copper mould tubing, cylinder head gaskets, engine coolants and sealants, shock absorbers, PVC emulsions and synchroniser rings. He is also involved in water purification and sewage treatment plants. He is, he says, the first member of his family to show distinct entrepreneurial flair.

*Main Companies*
Anand Chang Yun Ltd. (synchroniser rings)
Anchemo Ltd. (PVC materials)
Anfilco Ltd. (filters)
Degrement India Ltd. (water treatment)
Euran Metals Ltd. (copper mouldings)
Gabriel India Ltd. (shock absorbers, bearings)
Perfect Circle Victor Ltd. (gaskets)
Purolator India Ltd. (filters)
**Value of group listed companies: $40 million**

Nearly fifty years ago, in southern India, **A. M. M. Arunachalam** started a company producing only bicycles and abrasives that has today led to the formation of the Murugappa group. One of the group's earliest companies was Tube Investments of India, a joint venture which today is the second largest manufacturer of bikes in India, with nearly a one-fifth share in the market. The family owns about 20 per cent of each company in the conglomerate but is trying to maintain management control and direction. Today the founder's son, **M. V. Arunachalam**, has taken over a substantial part of his father's management responsibilities. When the family left India upon Independence, they started to collect business opportunities in earnest wherever they found them. Since those days the group, which has a keen focus on export markets, has expanded into other areas, notably engineering, agribusiness and electronics. They also have a joint asset-management venture with the British 'royal' stockbrokers, Cazenove. The agribusiness arm grew out of the acquisition, fifteen years ago, of E. I. D. Parry, which was involved very early on with all aspects of the sugar industry. Its main business today is fertilisers. The family is also involved in tea and confectionery.

*Main Companies*
Amphotronix
Bharat Pulverising Mills
Carborundum Universal Ltd.
Cholamandalam Factoring
Cholamandalam Investment & Finance
Coromandel Fertilisers
Dhanyalakshmi
Eastern Abrasive
E. I. D. Parry (India) Ltd.
Mofussil Warehouse
Murugappa Morgan Thermal Ceramics
Parry & Co.
Parry Agro Industries Ltd.
Parrys Confectionery Ltd.
T. I. Diamond Chain
Teekay Investments
Tube Investments of India Ltd.
**Value of group listed companies: $180 million**

**Rahul Bajaj** and cousins **Shekhar, Niraj** and **Shishir Bajaj** and **Rajeev Shah** own, through joint shareholding, 100 per cent of the Bajaj group's investment companies. Best known for manufacturing scooters, India's favourite mode of transport, the Bajaj family owns outright over forty companies. The main company, Bajaj Auto Ltd., run personally by Rahul, is the world's fourth largest manufacturer in its sector. The group also operates a finance company to lend money to those wanting to buy their vehicles. Apart from vehicle production, the family has interests ranging from *ayurvedic* and naturopathic medicines to cotton trading, heavy engineering, consumer durables, steel, sugar and the travel business. Shishir is responsible for the management of the naturopathic medicine companies, as well as for Bajaj Hindustan Ltd., a major producer of sugar. The consumer electronics side is handled by Shekhar through Bajaj Electricals Ltd.

The Bajaj group is one of India's few real world leaders in one particular product. They are arguably the biggest and cheapest scooter-maker in the world, with the only real competition these days probably coming from China. For those investing in India, Bajaj has traditionally been a core holding and has performed very well. The company is now beginning to diversify into cars, which concerns some people, since it is not a Bajaj area of dominance or expertise so far. There is an American Depository Receipt for the stock, which trades at a significant premium to the local share price.

*Main Companies*
Bajaj Auto Ltd.
Bajaj Auto Finance Ltd.
Bajaj Electricals Ltd.
Bajaj Hindustan Ltd.
Bajaj Shevashram Ltd.
Maharashtra Scooters Ltd.
Mukand Ltd.
**Value of group listed companies: approximately $1.8 billion**

**Subash Chandra**
Chandra pioneered lamitubes for use in the retailing of toothpaste, and Essel World and Zee TV. This makes him largely responsible, according to many in India, for the revolutions the country has seen in both TV and consumerism. The group has ambitious satellite telecommunications plans.

*Main Company*
Essel Packaging

The largest Sony dealership in the world, in terms of volume of branded goods sold, is in the hands of a new maharajah, **Manu Chhabria**, of the Chhabria Electronics Group. Through the Dubai-based Jumbo Group and the Indian company Shaw Wallace – the Chhabria corporate vehicle in India – Manu and his family are today also involved in distilleries and breweries, agricultural and consumer products, yeast, leather, rubber and engineering, as well as investment and the original electronics division. Getting into brewing and the production of alcoholic beverages in India is no mean feat: it is perhaps the most complex of bureaucratic processes, in an already overly paper-bound society, involving the establishment of different companies in different states, each with the appropriate paperwork and connections. Chhabria's company works with an individual in each relevant province, and provides umbrella marketing for the company's brands.

*Main Companies*
Shaw Wallace & Co.
Balbir, Central Cruickshank, Kerala, Maharashtra, Pampasar, Salamdar (distilleries)
Charminar, East Coast, Haryana, Haywards, Mehra, SICA, SKOL (breweries)
Dunlop India (rubber products)
Genelec, New Video, Nihon Electronics, Orson Video, Shaw Wallace Electronics (electronics)
Gordon Woodroffe (leather)
Hindustan Dorr Oliver Engineering
Indian Yeast
Mather & Platt Engineering
**Value of group listed companies: $250 million**

Together with the chairman, **C. H. Choksey**, three families are involved in the management of one of India's largest paint manufacturers, Asian Paints Ltd. The company is twenty-ninth in India in terms of total market capitalisation, and has a market share in the industrial paint business of nearly 40 per cent, making it the country's second largest in the sector. The management made a key decision early on to take their business global, and set up foreign subsidiaries in countries throughout the Pacific Rim. Choksey started operations originally in 1945, together with **Suryakant Dani**. Also in the business are the **Choksi** and **Vakil** families. C. H.'s eldest son **Atul C. Choksey**, is the managing director, while other key family members in the day-to-day management of the companies are **Ashwin C. Choksi, Ashwin S. Dani**, and **Abhay A. Vakil**. A team of professional managers from outside the families helps to run the business, and computerisation and automation also play their part, in the form of state-of-the-art methods of distribution and inventory systems. The company has some key international alliances which allow it to stay on top of the market: these include relationships with Devoe Marine Coatings of the US, Nippon Paints of Japan, Wacker Chemie of Germany and Sigma Coatings of the Netherlands.

*Main Companies*
Asian Paints Ltd. (India and overseas subsidiaries)

Pentasia Investments Ltd.
**Value of group listed companies: $330 million**

With many of the older family group companies, diversification is so extensive that simple categorisation according to sector is no longer possible. So it is with Dalmias. The group as a whole is making a courageous foray into world markets, particularly with their Malaysia-based palm oil refining interest, Twenty-First Century Oil Mills; their cotton weaving business in Turkey; and their trading companies in Singapore and New York. The two key players in the group are brothers **Sanjay** and **Anurag Dalmia** who control Gujarat Heavy Chemicals, GTC Industries and Dalmia Industries. These companies grew out of their father's share in Dalmia Dairy and a stake in GTC Industries, which was bought with compensation money for interests lost in Pakistan at the time of Partition. Although there are other family members involved in the business, today it is only Sanjay who is considered to be a substantial new maharajah. The group is powerful in a number of areas, including tobacco, chemicals, textiles, dairy products, telecommunications, power, explosives, biotechnology and the media.

*Main Companies*
Bharat Explosives
Dalmia Fresenius Medical
Dalmia Industries (dairy products)
Dalmia Industries (Nepal)
Dalmia Power Corporation
Dalmia Resorts
DSS Mobile Communications
GHCL Overseas
GTC Global
GTC Industries (tobacco and related products)
Gujarat Heavy Chemicals (soda ash)
India Telecomp
Odemis Textiles (Turkey)
Shree Menakshi Mills
Twenty-First Century Oil Mills (Malaysia)
**Value of group listed companies: approximately $65 million**

**Venugopal Dhoot** started in the electronic business dealing mostly in television and audio equipment through his listed company, Videocon International. Nowadays he is striving for more distant horizons in the fields of petroleum, power and telecommunications. He is also dipping his toes into financial waters, through a leasing operation which offers various forms of financing. Videocon was at one time a 'hot stock', which may have been due to overestimations of India's increasing affluence.

*Main Companies*
Videocon Appliances
Videocon International
Videocon Leasing & Industrial Finance
Videocon Narmada
Videocon Power
**Value of group listed companies: approximately $230 million**

From Maharashtra, **H. K. Firodia** and **N. K. Firodia** (who is now retired), together with their sons **Arun** and **Abhay**, manufacture the Luna, TFR, Spark and Safari motorcycles, have a scooter joint venture with Honda, make tractors and commercial vehicles, and manufacture gears in a collaboration with the German company, Zahnradfabrik Friedrichshafen A. G. They have a number of financing companies, all of which are designed to help the consumer in the purchase of their company products, and are starting to diversify into multimedia and interactive television.

*Main Companies*
Bajaj Tempo
Integrated Kinetic Finance
Jaya Hind Sciaky
Kinetic Capital Ltd.
Kinetic Communications
Kinetic Engineering Ltd.
Kinetic Motor Honda Ltd.
Tempo Finance (North)
Tempo Finance (West)
Twentieth-Century Kinetic Finance
ZF Steering Gear
**Value of group listed companies: approximately $195 million**

The Goenkas are a major if sometimes controversial force in Indian business. Their power, mostly exercised by **R. P. Goenka**, the present chairman, has come through the acquisition of a large number of licences, perhaps most notably for Searle, Bayer, Fujitsu, Sprint and Ricoh. They are involved in technology and communications, rubber, power, chemicals, utilities and services. While to some Goenka is a mere asset-stripper, to others he is the stuff of financial genius.

*Main Companies*
Asian Cables
Balagarh Power Supply
Bayer (India)
Benninger (India)
Carbon & Chemicals
Ceat Ltd.
Ceat Financial Services
Cellular Communication Services
CESC
Cescon Ltd.
FGP (India)
Fujitsu ICIM
Gramophone Co. of India
Harrisons Malayalam
India Polyfibres
KEC International
Mobile Telecoms
Nitel
Nodia Power Supply
Phillips Carbon Black
Raychem Technologies
RPG-BTP
RPG Cellular Services
RPG Paging Services
RPG Ricoh
RPG-RR Power Engineering
RPG Telecom
RPG V-Sat Services
SAE (India)
Searle (India)
South Asia Tyres

Spencer & Co.
Spentex Industries
Sprint-RPG
Sulzer (India)
Upcom Cables
**Value of group listed companies: approximately $565 million**

**Deshbandhu Gupta** is the brains behind the still small but significant listed Indian pharmaceutical company Lupin Laboratories, which has annual sales of well over $120 million, mostly from its tuberculosis medicines. Gupta, who struggled up and out of a far-flung Indian village to get where he is today, is working hard to broaden his business out into both China and the United States.

*Main Company*
Lupin Laboratories
**Value of listed company: approximately $4.5 million**

**Sushilkumar Handa** is a chartered accountant and management graduate. Although he has no background whatsoever in pharmaceuticals or the healthcare industry, he has, together with his younger brother, **Sunilkumar**, and their uncle, **Baldevraj**, taken award-winning company Core Healthcare forward since its start-up less than ten years ago to become the largest manufacturer of IV fluids in India. They have ambitious but realisable expansion plans for operations in China, Dubai, Sri Lanka and Vietnam, and want to achieve global dominance in intravenous fluids. They also aim to branch out into other areas of production, and have already made a start with products for dentistry and intensive care. Their stock, perhaps surprisingly, has until recently been a major underperformer.

*Main Companies*
Core Biotech Ltd.
Core Healthcare Ltd.
Core International Ltd.
**Value of group listed companies: approximately $180 million**

**Shahnaz Husain** is the CEO of her Indian cosmetics company which produces 450 products and is said to have captured 80 per cent of the domestic market. Her achievements brought her to the attention of the American publication *Success* magazine who named her 'the world's greatest woman entrepreneur' in 1996. She started producing *ayurvedic* medicines in her own kitchen but these days is said to have reached the dizzy heights of supplying NASA astronauts with samples to use during flights in space. Her products are also said to have found favour with Diana, Princess of Wales who is reputed to use the company's blue kohl eyeliner.

*Main Company*
Shahnaz Herbals
**Value of listed company: approximately $100 million**

**D. Jayavarthanavelu** and his uncle **G.K. Sundaram** run the Lakshmi group's textile-related operations, set up over 30 years ago. The family mostly produces heavy machinery for the industry but also makes looms and is recently diversifying into investment and finance.

*Main Companies*
Lakshmi Electrical Control Systems Ltd.
Lakshmi Machine Works Ltd.
Siscol Ltd.
Super Sales Agencies Ltd.
Textool Co. Ltd.
**Value of group listed companies: approximately US$320 million**

**O. P. Jindal,** together with his sons, **Prithvi Raj, Sajjan, Ratan,** and **Naveen**, run their company very professionally. They bear in mind a popular saying 'Where there is steel there is Jindal' and try to develop and source all technology and materials in India itself. Starting out virtually in a shed at the bottom of his garden, O. P. now finds himself running a conglomerate with a reputation for very high standards. B.C. Jindal, one of O.P.'s brothers, runs a separate empire said to be worth something in the region of US$160 million.

*Main Companies*
Jindal Iron & Steel Co.
Jindal Strips Ltd.
Saw Pipes Ltd.
**Value of group listed companies: approximately US$895 million**

**B. N. Kalyani** is the second generation in the family commercial forgings business and was educated mainly in the US. The firm, which was started by Dr. Neelkanth Kalyani, is currently setting up a steel plant but also has major joint ventures with Rockwell Intl. and with General Motors, Ford, Mitsubishi and Mercedes Benz for automotive related business and with Sharp for electronics.

*Main Companies*
Bharat Forge Ltd.
Kalyani Forge Ltd.
Kalyani Steels Ltd.
**Value of group listed companies: approximately US$45 million**

**B. M. Khaitain** works out of Calcutta, whilst his colleagues, the **Magors**, are based in the United Kingdom. In its most recent incarnation, this business venture began some thirty years ago, when Khaitain, a supplier of tea chests, acquired the Williamson Major interest. At the moment, more than half of their daily business activity is in engineering and construction, but they are still heavily involved in tea – mostly from Assam and West Bengal – and in packaging.

*Main Companies*
Bishnauth Tea Co.
George Williamson (Assam)
Mcleod Russel (India)
Williamson Major & Co.
*Other Companies*
Eveready Industries India
India Foils
Kilburn Chemicals
Kilburn Engineering
Kilburn Reprographics
Light Metal Industries
Standard Batteries
Williamson Financial Services
Worthington Pump
**Value of group listed companies: approximately $450 million**

Based in Madras but originally from the Punjab, **Ravi Prakash Khemka**, a former scrap-metal dealer, and his sons are said to be India's most viable takeover tycoons. They have stellar ambitions for a satellite television channel, and are also dabbling in cement, insurance and pharmaceuticals. At the end of 1995 they launched a hostile bid for the Modi family's airline, Modiluft. The Khemkas have their critics at home and abroad, although they are popular with those who would like to jump on the family's bandwagon of success that started rolling with liberalisation in 1991.

*Main Companies*
NEPC-Agro Foods
NEPC-Micon
NEPC Paper & Board
NEPC Textiles
Skyline NEPC
**Value of group listed companies: $136 million**

Pune-based **Vijay Kirloskar** and his nephews **Atul, Sanjay, Rahul** and **Vikram** are perhaps best known for their joint venture with the American company, Kirloskar Cummins, renowned for its internal combustion engines. Although the family are no longer involved in the management of the company, they still retain an equity stake. The Kirloskars are actively engaged in a number of different sectors: Vijay himself has interests in investment, consultancy and leasing, while the nephews each have their own commercial concerns in compressors, engines, motors and pumps.

*Main Companies*
G. G. Dandekar Machine Works
Kirloskar Brothers
Kirloskar Copeland
Kirloskar EBARA
Kirloskar Electric
Kirloskar Electrodyne
Kirloskar Ferrous Industries
Kirloskar Investments
Kirloskar Leasing & Finance
Kirloskar Oil Engines
Kirloskar Pneumatic
Kirloskar Warner Swasey

Mysore Kirloskar
Shivaji Works
**Value of group listed companies: approximately $115 million**

**Arvind Lalbhai** and his son **Samveg** run the Lalbhai family group, which includes Arvind Mills, the largest producer in India – and one of the ten largest in the world – of indigo-dyed denim fabrics. The family are not new to the textile business; the company is currently celebrating its centenary of involvement with the industry, although Arvind Mills was not officially founded till 1937. Management policy for the last ten years has been to concentrate on the export market, a decision that has clearly paid off. Their main focus these days is not on Indian textiles, but on the highest-quality cotton fabrics. Working together with father and son on a daily basis are Arvind's brothers, **Niranjan** and **S. N.**, and his nephew, **Sanjay**. They are one of the most celebrated Indian companies and a very important producer of denim, and are best known in the outside world as the manufacturers of Lee jeans and Arrow brand shirts.

*Main Companies*
Amal Rasayan Ltd.
Anagram Finance Ltd. (leasing, HP)
Anil Starch Products Ltd.
Arvind Clothing Ltd. (Arrow brand shirts)
Arvind Mills Ltd.
Arvind Polycot Ltd.
Arvind Worldwide Inc. NY (marketing in the USA)
Arvind Worldwide (M) Inc. (marketing in the European Union and the USA)
Atul Products Ltd.
**Value of group listed companies: approximately $415 million**

The **Mafatial** family business started out nearly 100 years ago like so many in India in textiles, but today has branched out into a number of different areas including natural gas, plastics, information technology, chemicals and the financial sector. While valued as a whole as indicated below, the three brothers, **Arvind, Yogindra** and **Rasesh**, have run their own companies independently since splitting off about 15 years ago.

**Arvind N. Mafatial & H. A. Mafatial**

*Main Companies*
Gujarat Gas Company
Mafatial Fine Spinning & Manufacturing Company
Mafatial Industries Ltd.
NOCIL Ltd.

**Rasesh N. Mafatial & P. Mafatial**
G L Rexroth Industries Ltd.
Sandeep Holdings
Standard Industries Ltd.

**Yogindra N. Mafatial & A. Y. Mafatial**
Indian Dyestuff Industries Ltd.
Mafatial Dyes & Chemicals Ltd.
Mahaamba Investment
**Value of group listed companies: approximately US$725 million**

**Harish** and **Keshub Mahindra** became involved in the family business in Bombay about forty years ago and since then have taken the group from strength to strength. Their most successful product – and certainly the one for which they are best known – is their multi-seater Armada jeep, which they sell not only in India but on the African continent as well. Their name is often put forward by their peers as a shining example of the way successful business should be conducted today. Moving on from mere vehicle production, the Mahindras are now dabbling in software and the hotel industry. They have a joint venture with Ford to make Escorts, and other partnerships with British Telecom, Days Inn, Otis Elevator, Schindling and A. G. Vickers.

*Main Company*
Mahindra & Mahindra
*Subsidiary Companies*
Mahindra-British Telecom
Mahindra Engineering and Chemical Products
Mahindra Exports
Mahindra Hellenic Auto Industries S. A.
Mahindra Holdings & Finance
Mahindra Information Technology Services
Mahindra Realty & Infrastructure Developers

Mahindra Sintered Products
Mahindra Steel Service Centre
Mahindra USA Inc.
*Associated Companies*
Dr Beck & Company (India)
EAC Graphics (India)
International Instruments
M&M Contek
M&M Financial Services
M&M Sona Steering
Mahindra Mathew Construction Co.
Mahindra Towers Services
Mahindra Ugine Steel Co.
Otis Elevator Company (India)
Roplas (India)
Siro Plast
Vickers Systems International
**Value of group listed companies: approximately $500 million**

India's liquor barons are the relatives of the late **Vittal Mallya**, who was succeeded as head of this massive drinks empire by his international jetset son **Vijay**. The leading brand for the company, who have a joint venture with United Distillers, is Kingfisher beer, which is the country's best-seller and is drunk widely overseas. Nowadays the business involvement ranges from electronics and construction to fertilisers and food.

*Main Company*
United Breweries
*Other Companies*
Air Control
BDA
Beacon Carbons & Electricals
Beacon Process
Beacon Tileman
Best & Crompton Engineering
Esquire Engineering & Construction
Herbertsons
McDowell & Co.
Mangalore Chemicals & Fertilisers

UB Engineering
**Value of group listed companies: approximately $100 million**

**M. L. Mittal**, who is in his mid-sixties, and his sons **L. N.** and **P. K. Mittal**, have been among the principal players in India's steel business for more than forty years. The company also has international operations in Trinidad & Tobago, Mexico and Indonesia. In 1986 they were the first people in India to produce thin gauge galvanized steel sheets, which were manufactured in a joint venture with the Japanese Nippon Denro Manufacturing Company Ltd. They have also produced India's first coated steel sheets within the last five years.

*Main Companies*
Ispat Alloys Ltd.
Nippon Denro Ispat Ltd.
*Other Companies*
Gontermann-Peipers India Ltd.
**Value of group listed companies: approximately $165 million**

One of India's largest textile empires is that controlled by the somewhat controversial Delhi-based Modi family, specifically by three brothers, **G. M. Modi** and his two younger brothers, **K. N.** and **K. K.** The management baton has now passed to G. M.'s five sons, who work in concert with their cousins. The original business was clothes-related, but the group has long since diversified, into finance, software, tyre production and tobacco, as well as office equipment. K. K. Modi has a very strong relationship with Walt Disney of the United States, and with a number of other film companies and distributors. He owns a two-thirds share in International Research Park Laboratories, and a one-third share in Godfrey Phillips India, with interests in tobacco and tea. B. K. Modi has relationships of note with Champion sparkplugs, Olivetti, Telstra and Xerox. Problems have occasionally arisen over the Modis' relations with foreign investors, causing the group to be very unpopular with a number of Indian financial institutions: their association with auction company Sotheby's, for example, fell apart very early on. However, as one partnership disintegrates, another seems to appear, the latest being AIG, who will work with the Modis in the telecommunications business.

*Main Companies*
Bihar Sponge Iron Ltd.
Godfrey Phillips (India) Ltd.
Modi Alkalis & Chemicals Ltd.
Modi Cement Ltd.
Modi Champion Ltd.
Modi GBC Ltd.
Modi Industries Ltd.
Modi Olivetti Ltd.
Modi Rubber Ltd.
Modi Spinning & Weaving Ltd.
Modi Threads Ltd.
Modi Xerox Ltd.
Modiluft Ltd.
Modipon Ltd.
Modistone Ltd.
SBEC Ltd.
**Value of group listed companies: approximately $255 million**

**Brimohan Lall Munjal** is a first-generation entrepreneur who started out over forty-five years ago in the Punjab city of Ludhiana, with his brothers **Dayanand, Om Prakash** and **Satyanand**. From being a small manufacturer of bicycle components, the group has grown into a major producer of motorcycles, specifically through their Hero and Majestic companies. Today they own the world's single largest bicycle manufacturer – turning out over three and a half million a year – and India's largest producer of motorcycles. Hero Honda enjoys a 50 per cent market share for its products. In terms of international partnerships, Majestic Auto, which started out twenty years ago making Peugeot-style mopeds, today has a business agreement with BMW of Germany for 650cc motorcycles and cars, and has an association, too, with Porsche. The Munjals are also working on a number of schemes for moving into China. The family have contributed to the building of several institutions for the development of Ludhiana.

*Main Companies*
Gujarat Cycles Ltd.
Hero Honda Motors Ltd.
Majestic Auto Ltd.

Munjal Showa Ltd.
**Value of group listed companies: approximately $175 million**

**Narayana R. Murthy,** Infosys, see page 107.

**T. P. G. Nambiar** is the chairman and head of the thirty-year-old
BPL Group, makers of electronic and white goods. The company
originally started out as a joint venture but flourished and went on to
commercial independence. The patriarch works together with his
son, **Ajit**, his daughter, **Anju**, his son-in-law **Rajeev Chandrashe-
kar** and a brother-in-law, **Viswanath Nambiar**. His son and heir is
mostly in charge of the engineering and automation parts of the
group. One division, BPL Telecom, has a joint venture with the US
telecommunications company US West.

*Main Companies*
BPL Automation
BPL Engineering Ltd.
BPL Mobile Communications
BPL Power
BPL Refrigeration
BPL Sanyo Finance
BPL Sanyo Technologies
BPL Utilities and Appliances Ltd.
BPL Systems & Projects
BPL Telecom
Dynamic Electronics
**Value of group listed companies: approximately $100 million**

The Piramal brothers' business empire began with the interest of the
elder, **M. Piramal**, in spinning and weaving mills, which he then
broadened to include a company producing electronic gears. His
younger brother, **G. Piramal**, works together with his wife, Urvi,
and their two sons in perhaps the more interesting area of the group,
which is involved in a variety of sectors, from healthcare to a partnership with the US company Mattel to produce toys.

*Main Companies*
Blow Past Toys
DGP Windsor
Electric Control Gears

G. P. Electrics
Kemp & Co.
Mattel Toys
Morarjee Gocoldas Spinning & Weaving
Nicholas Piramal
Piramal Healthcare
Piramal Spinning & Weaving Mills
Universal Luggage
VIP Industries
**Value of group listed companies: approximately $300 million**

**Ramasubrahmaneya Rajha** is CEO of a group which includes Madras Cements, Ramco Industries, Ramco Systems, Rajapalayam Mills, and Ramaraju Surgical Cotton Mills amongst others. The group was founded by his father, Ramasamy, in 1938. There has lately been a big expansion in the cement sector of the business, but Rajha's US-educated son is keen to take the group further into software.

One of the predominant new maharajahs in the pharmaceuticals sector is the exuberant extrovert **K. Anji Reddy**, a first-generation entrepreneur who together with **M. P. Chary** set up Dr Reddy's Laboratories Ltd. Working with them, and sharing the responsibility for day-to-day management, are **K. Satish Reddy**, who studied both in India and the US, **A. Subba Reddy**, and **G. V. Prasad**. The company is the largest producer in India and the largest exporter in the world of ibuprofen. The key to success in this sector till very recently has been the ability of Indian manufacturers to spin clones of existing overseas patents at lower cost, under the protection of Indian patent laws – which protect only processes, not the products themselves. The company does, however, produce its own formulations for nearly half of its products and is investing heavily in research and development, mindful of the fact that the protection afforded by these patent laws will come to an end in the year 2005, India having agreed to level the playing field for the international producers. This company is a good example of how successful Indian businesses can become at the less glamorous end of the manufacturing process: they may not be in the headlines for having developed exciting new drugs, but they are extremely skilful at manufacturing them at low cost.

*Main Companies*
Cheminor Drugs Ltd.
Dr Reddy's Laboratories Ltd.
Globe Organics Ltd.
Kesoram Industries Ltd.
Standard Equity Fund Ltd.
Trident Organics PVT Ltd.
**Value of group listed companies: $150 million**

**Ravi** and **Sashi Ruia** control one of the most important conglom-erates in India and are involved in oil and gas, shipping, steel, telecommunications, and financial services. They were also thought to be exploring a venture into India's first California-style theme park. Both of Sashi's sons, **Prashant** and **Anshuman** are actively engaged in the business.

*Main Companies*
Essar Gujarat
Essar Oil
Essar Power
Essar Shipping
India Securities
South India Shipping Corporation
**Value of group listed companies: approximately US$530 million**

**Ram Sharan Sanghi**, together with **Anand Prakash, Sudhir Ravi** and **Gireesh Sanghi** own Sanghi Polyester Ltd. which is India's second largest manufacturer of polyester filament yarn, a key ingredient in the country's modern textile industry.

*Main Companies*
Sanghi Industries Ltd.
Sanghi Plantation Ltd
Sanghi Polyesters
Sanghi Spinners
Sanghi Synthetics
Sanghi Textile Processors
**Value of group listed companies: approximately US$150 million**

**K. M. Sheth** is the overall boss of the Great Eastern Shipping Company, the largest private sector shipping company in India. He works on a day-to-day basis in the 50-year old company with his sons, Vijay, 40, and Bharat, 37, and also with his nephew, Ghanshyam, aged 39. The latter is managing the group's foray into real estate.

*Main Company*
The Great Eastern Shipping Co. Ltd.
**Value of group listed companies: approximately US$750 million**

It was the late **Sir Lala Shriram** of Delhi who pioneered the companies that now make up the DCM group, and his heirs **Shri Dhar, Dr Bansi Dhar** and **Bharat Ram** and **Charat Ram** oversee all operations between them. They run the gamut of industry from textiles to engineering, and from optical products to nylon yarns, sugar and car assembly with Honda.

*Main Companies*
DCM Ltd.
DCM Shriram Consolidated
DCM Shriram Industries
Daurala Organics
Shriram Industrial Enterprises
**Value of group listed companies: approximately US$380 million**

Less than five years ago, internecine warfare broke out between **Bhai Mohan Singh**, the founder of the Ranbaxy pharmaceutical company, and his children over who should own which of his assets. The fight was keen, since Ranbaxy is the leader in domestic production of antibiotics and anti-bacterial products. The company has focused on the USA as a market for its generic drug formulations, and on mainland China and the countries of the former Soviet Union and Eastern Bloc for its branded products. There is a lot at stake. The eventual victor was **Parvinder Singh**, an American-educated pharmacist, with a Master's Degree from Washington State and a doctorate from the University of Michigan. Dr Parvinder has a distinct fondness for research and development, and is personally involved in taking the company forward by designing new pharmaceutical formulations. He works with his companies' professional managers to make sure that the drugs are marketed and distributed with the maximum efficiency. He has clear global designs, illustrated by a number of strategic international alliances. Mr Singh senior has been moved sideways out of management and has been given the distinctive title of 'Chairman Emeritus'.

*Main Companies*
Eli Lilly Ranbaxy Ltd.
Ranbaxy-Genpharm Ltd., Canada
Ranbaxy Guangzhou (China) Ltd.
Ranbaxy (Hong Kong) Ltd.
Ranbaxy Inc.
Ranbaxy Laboratories Ltd.
Ranbaxy (Malaysia) Sdn. Bhd.
Ranbaxy (Netherlands) B. V.
Ranbaxy (Thailand) Co. Ltd.
Ranmax Laboratories (Nigeria) Ltd.
**Value of group listed companies: $750 million**

**Vijaypat Singhania**, together with his brothers, **Dr Gaur Hari Singhania** and **H.S. Singhania** own interests in companies which together make up the J.K. Group, called after its founder, their father the late **Juggilal Kamlapat** and is mostly involved in cement, paper, power, sugar, textiles and telecommunications.

*Main Companies*
J.K. Chemicals
J.K. Synthetics
Jaykayorg AG
Raymond Synthetics
Raymond Woollen Mills (Kenya)
**Value of group listed companies: approximately US$650 million**

**Venu Srinivasan** is the CEO of TVS Suzuki, connected with the Sundaram group of companies. Also related to his operations is the T S Santhanan branch of the group, which owns Sundaram Finance, Wheels India and Impal. Another part of the same TVS group owns Sundaram Fasteners, a favourite stock with US investors.

*Main Company*
TVS Suzuki
**Value of group listed companies: $560 million**

**Nusli Wadia**'s business started originally over a hundred years ago, with the Bombay Dyeing Company (textiles) and the Bombay Burmah Trading Company (tea and coffee). The company has long since moved on from the strict confines of the textile sector to include interests in food processing, building and construction, chemicals, metals, dental products and precision instruments.

*Main Companies*
Bombay Burmah Trading Corporation
Bombay Dyeing Co. Ltd.
Britannia
Citurgia Biochemicals
Dental Products of India
Gherzi Eastern
Medical Microtechnology
National Peroxide
Wadia BSN India
**Value of group listed companies: $400 million**

Other names worth noting but which it is too early to assess to any degree of commercial accuracy are the **Rane (approximate value of group listed companies: $95 million)** and **Amalgamations** groups, two prominent Madras corporate families who are involved in auto components and other sectors. Also notable are the **Doshis** at Premier Auto whose company has a joint venture with Peugeot. The **Godrej** family, whose wealth and share ownership is almost impossible to verify, are very important players in everything from soaps to office automation.

**Bollywood**, the prolific Bombay dominated Indian film world is more than worthy of inclusion for its creation of a number of significant personalities. Since *Alam Ara* (1931, India) which was the first all-singing, all-dancing Bombay talkie, the industry has progressed to include such world-class greats as **Satyajit Ray**. Ray was born in 1921 into a cultivated Bengali family and was influenced in early life by the great poet Rabindranath Tagore, and by his own father

Sukumar, a noted Bengali writer. He became acquainted with the French director Jean Renoir when Renoir was making his film *The River* in Calcutta. Encouraged by Renoir, Ray started work on *Pather Panchali* (Song of the Road, 1955). This film, the first of the Apu trilogy based on novels by the Bengali writer Bibhuti Bhushan Banerji, was completed on a shoestring budget. At the 1956 Cannes Film Festival it was voted the 'best human document' shown.

Other leading industry figures include **Shyam Benegal** (*Ankur,* The Seedling, 1974), **Govind Nihalani** (*Ardh Satya*) and **Mrinal Sen**, like Ray a product of the Calcutta film society movement. Among the promising younger film makers are **Ketan Mehta** (*Bhavni Bhavai*, A Folk Tale, 1980), and **Kundan Shah** (*Jaane Bhi Do Yaaro*). Eclectic, dynamic and inventive, their work deals with issues ranging from housing problems and casteism to the lust for money in the corridors of power.

# Pakistan

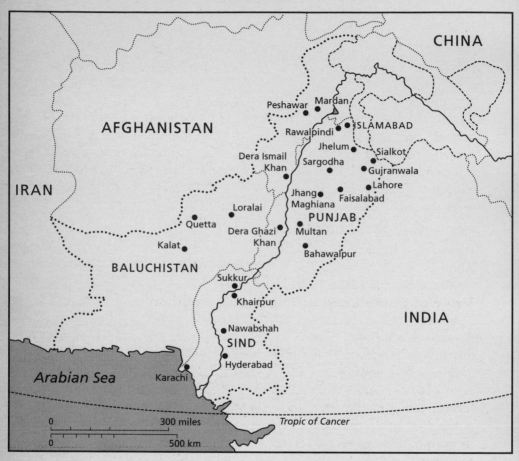

Chapter 3

# Who's Really Who in Pakistan*

The main business of **Mian Abdullah**'s Sapphire Group is the manufacture and sale of spun cotton yarn. Sapphire Fibre is a spinning unit with an installed capacity of 59,584 spindles, and Abdullah is also adding in a knitting and dyeing unit. The original company, Sapphire Textile Mills, incorporated in 1969, is also a spinning unit, with an installed capacity of 101,000 spindles.

*Main Companies*
Reliance Cotton
Sapphire Fibre
Sapphire Textile Mills
**Value of group listed companies: $60 million**

**Rashid Abdullah**'s United Distributors group is in the business of distributing consumer – mainly pharmaceutical goods – throughout Pakistan. His companies have all been in existence for some time now and are considered to be managed with a high degree of professionalism. He also has substantial holdings in a number of unlisted companies in the pharmaceutical, consumer product and computer industries. The most significant of these is Searle Pakistan, whose products Candarel and Hydrillin are among the top-selling names in their fields in Pakistan.

*Main Company*
UDL Modaraba

*Source: Company Annual Reports

*Other Companies*
Gillette Pakistan
Searle Pakistan
UDL Industries
United Distribution
**Value of group listed companies: $62 million**

Adamjee Insurance, run by **Hanif Adamjee**, is the number-one non-life insurance concern in Pakistan. It has a number of branches throughout the country, as well as several overseas offices. The group was started by Sir Adamjee Haji Dawood at the beginning of the twentieth century, and the Adamjee Insurance Co. Ltd. was incorporated in 1960, achieving a listing on the Karachi Stock Exchange the following year. The history of the company has not been without setbacks, however: at the beginning of the 1970s, the nationalisation of Pakistan's entire life insurance business forced the family into diversification. However, with proposed government reforms for the industry announced recently, the Dawoods plan to use their historical position to make a fresh start in that sector.

*Main Company*
Adamjee Insurance
**Value of listed company: approximately $83 million**

**Sheikh Mukhtar Ahmed**, who is considered by the market to be the maharajah of the Ibrahim Group, is a recent member of the clan of Pakistan's new maharajahs. The major interest of his companies lies in the manufacture of cotton yarn and synthetic fibres, and Ibrahim Fibres has gone into the manufacture of the all-important polyester staple fibre (PSF). Production of this is based in Shahkot, in Faisalabad, and when it reaches full production capacity the plant should be able to turn out around 60,000 tonnes per annum. Another company, Ibrahim Energy, runs a power plant that feeds the group's textile mills.

*Main Companies*
First Ibrahim Modaraba
Ibrahim Leasing
*Subsidiary Companies*
A. A. Textile Mills
Ibrahim Fibres

Ibrahim Textile Mills
Zainab Textile Mills
**Value of group listed companies: approximately $115 million**

**Syed Babur Ali**'s main business is the printing and packaging of consumer and industrial products. He is considered to be entrepreneurial and commercially forward-looking. His flagship company, Packages, was established forty years ago as a joint venture with Akerland Rausing, a Swedish company, and now produces its own board and inks. It recently launched a $3 million expansion programme to modernise the plant. Through the Treet Corporation, Ali manufactures razor blades and is dominant in the domestic market. His stable includes the Hoechst, Nestlé and Siemens alliances for Pakistan, and the group also accommodates an insurance company, an investment bank, and a small commodity trading company.

*Main Companies*
First International Investment Bank
*Other Companies*
Hoechst Pakistan
International General Insurance
Nestlé Milk Pak
Packages
Siemens Engineering Pak
Treet Corporation
Wazir Ali Oils
Zulfiqar Industries
**Value of group listed companies: approximately $290 million**

The Bawany family's main business is the sugar industry. One of the oldest groups in Pakistan, today it is the third generation of the family in whose hands the management lies. The three individuals most closely involved in the business are **Amin, Yahya** and **Zakari Bawany**, and although their companies do not constitute one cohesive business group, the family ties are very strong, and frequent consultations are made between them. Zakari's Pioneer Cables manufactures electric cables of varying sizes, mostly for the local market, while Yahya Bawany Air Products essentially fills canisters with compressed air for hospitals. The Bawanys' sugar companies manufacture not only sugar itself, but also a number of sugar-based products.

*Main Companies*
Al-Asif Sugar Mills
Annoor Textile
Bawany Air Products
Bawany Sugar Mills
Farhan Sugar Mills
Latif Jute
Pioneer Cables Ltd.
**Value of group listed companies: approximately $23 million**

**Ahmed Dawood** is one of Pakistan's senior industrialists: Dawood Cotton, his first listed company, started operations in 1953. Dawood Hercules is considered to be a blue-chip stock in the chemicals and pharmaceuticals sector. The company was incorporated in 1968 by an arrangement between Dawood and Hercules of the US, and is now the major manufacturer of fertilisers in Pakistan: the plant has a total manufacturing capacity of 423,000 tonnes of urea per annum.

*Main Companies*
Burewalla Textiles
Dawood Cotton
Dawood Hercules
Dilon Ltd.
Lawrencepur Textiles
Transpak Corporation
*Other Company*
First DG Modaraba
**Value of group listed companies: approximately $100 million**

Although **Siddiq Dawood**, brother of Ahmed, established his financial services group independently of his family, the two brothers are considered very much a group by the stock exchange. Siddiq began his operations only nine years ago with the foundation of First BRR Capital Modaraba.

*Main Companies*
First BRR Capital Modaraba
Second BRR Capital Modaraba
*Other Company*
Orient Insurance
**Value of group listed companies: approximately $16 million**

**Dewan Zia-ur-Rehman Farooqui**, the second generation in management in his family business, is a big player in the textile industry, through the manufacture of both cotton and synthetic fibres. The Dewan family is considered to run one of the most shareholder-friendly businesses in the country, and they are thus very well regarded. The group's first listed company was Dewan Mushtaq Textile Mills, which was founded in 1971. Dewan Salman Fibre has the distinction of being the first Pakistani company to successfully raise funds through a Euro Convertible Bond ($45 million). The company was formed in collaboration with the Mitsubishi Corporation of Japan and Sam Yang of South Korea, and is currently the largest producer of polyester staple fibre (PSF) in the country. Dewan Salman completed its PSF plant in record time, and an expansion has since doubled its capacity. The group is one of two companies (the other is ICI) to be given the go-ahead by the government for the construction of a PTA (Purified Terephthalic Acid, used in the construction of synthetic textiles) plant in Pakistan, and when this is completed it will be one of the most integrated PSF manufacturers in Pakistan.

*Main Companies*
Dewan Khalid Textile
Dewan Mushtaq Textile
Dewan Textile Mills
Dewan Salman Fibre
Dewan Sugar
**Value of group listed companies: approximately $600 million**

**Sheikh Enam Elahi** is not a major player in terms of market capitalisation, but the family from which he comes is an interesting one. They have been in the textile industry for over a decade, and have a fast-growing reputation. Their main business is spun cotton yarn.

*Main Companies*
Elahi Cotton
Elahi Spinning
Elcot Spinning
Taj Textiles
**Value of group listed companies: approximately $7 million**

The main business of **Mohammad Farooque**'s companies, the

Ghulam Farooque Group, is cement. The flagship of the company, Cherat Cement, was Pakistan's first private-sector cement plant. Production is based in the north of the country, where demand currently outstrips supply. After closure for expansion, the plant has recommenced operations, increasing its capacity from 360,000 to 620,000 tonnes per annum. Cherat Papersack, Farooque's paper and board company, is in reality a cement bag manufacturer which complements its sister concern as well as selling its products to other businesses in the region. There are plans to construct its own captive power plant, which will be floated as a separate company. Mirpurkhas Sugar is a significant and highly professional part of the conglomerate which in fact owns and manages the other companies in the group.

*Main Companies*
Cherat Cement
Cherat Papersack
Mirpurkhas Sugar
**Value of group listed companies: approximately $115 million**

The Habib family were once a combined force in Pakistan business, but since three of the brothers broke away and went their separate commercial ways, this is no longer the case. The three individual groups are the Dawood Habib Group, run by **Ali S. Habib**; the Rafiq Habib Group, run by **Rafiq Habib**; and the Industries of Habib, which is headed by **Ghaffar A. Habib**.

The main company for the Dawood Habib Group is the Indus Motor Company. With a market capitalisation of $48.33 million, the company assembles and supplies Toyota cars in Pakistan, and has an 80 per cent market share of both 1300cc and light commercial vehicles. In the financial sector, the group's Bank Al-Habib was set up as part of the government's deregulation of the banking sector, and there is also an involvement in insurance through Habib General. In terms of manufacturing, the Dawood Habib group owns the Habib Sugar Mills, the Baluchistan Particle & Board company and Baluchistan Glass, manufacturers of glass and ceramics.

Ghaffar A. Habib, chairman of the Industries of Habib, runs Habib Arcady, a sugar company. The other main business in his group is Haydary Construction. Rafiq Habib is involved in the financial services sector with the First Habib Modaraba and the Metropolitan

Bank, which is now among the top five commercial banks in the country in terms of profitability. Together with the Al-Futtaim Group of the Middle East he also runs the motor components company Agriauto Industries. Other interests are in cables and electrical components, synthetics, jute, paper and board, glass and ceramics and chemicals and pharmaceuticals.

*Main Companies*
First Habib Modaraba
Habib Arcady
Haydary Construction
Indus Motor Company
Metropolitan Bank
*Other Companies*
Agriauto Industries
Auvitronics
Baluchistan Foundry
Dynopak
Pak Jute Synthetics
Pak Papersack Corporation
Polypropylene
Shabbir Tiles & Ceramics
Thal Jute Mills
**Value of group listed companies: approximately $190 million**

**Akbar Ali Hashwani** and **Sadrudin Hashwani**, American-educated brothers, together run the Hashoo Group. The group is involved in a number of different businesses, ranging from steel and batteries to insurance and hotels. The brothers are the owners and operators of some 60 per cent of the Marriott chain of hotels in Pakistan, and also run the Pearl Continental chain. The Hashwanis' automobile battery business, which controls well over two-thirds of the market, is managed by Arif Hashwani, a nephew.

*Main Companies*
Automotive Battery
Exide Pakistan Ltd.
Hashoo Steel
Landmark Spinning
New Jubilee Insurance
Pakistan Services

Regent Textile Mills
**Value of group listed companies: approximately $40 million**

**Khawaja Mohammed Jawed**'s main business is textiles and the textile-based industries, although he has of late been diversifying into cement and financial services. The family has been involved in the textile industry since the time of Partition, when they migrated from East Pakistan (now Bangladesh) to Pakistan. While the power behind the group is Khawaja Mohammed, the company was founded by the four Jawed brothers, all of whom work together in handling the affairs of their businesses. They are amongst the most respected groups in the country.

One of the Jaweds' companies, Dhan Fibres Ltd., is the second largest producer of polyester staple fibre in Pakistan. Not long ago, under a government privatisation scheme, the group also acquired Dandot Cement, whose production is being expanded from 1,700 to 2,000 tonnes per day, while Chakwal Cement, when it reaches full production capacity, will be one of the largest producers of cement in Pakistan. The group has recently moved into commercial banking, with the Platinum Commercial Bank.

*Main Companies*
Amin Spinning
Chakwal Cement
Chakwal Spinning
Dandot Cement
Dhan Fibres, Synthetic & Rayon
Kohinoor Spinning
Mahmood Textile
Platinum Commercial Bank
Yousuf Weaving
**Value of group listed companies: approximately $170 million**

**Mazaar Karim**'s Crescent Group is involved in banking, textiles, financial services, leasing, sugar, paper and board, engineering and jute. Operations began in 1959 with the Crescent Textile Mills, and today they are amongst the largest industrial groups in Pakistan. The companies are professionally managed by siblings of the two brothers who started the business, and they also employ a number of highly professional technicians and other staff, most of whom have

72

been educated abroad. Crescent Investment Bank, currently the most profitable investment bank in Pakistan, has joined forces with Morgan Stanley Asset Management to form International Asset Management, which acts as the advisor to the Pakistan Growth Fund. The Crescent Group has the distinction of having the country's most diversified list of companies.

*Main Companies*
Crescent Boards
Crescent Investment Bank
Crescent Jute Products
Crescent Leasing
Crescent Modaraba
Crescent Spinning Mills
Crescent Steel & Allied
Crescent Sugar
Crescent Textile
Crescent Textile Mills
Elite Textile
First Elite Modaraba
First Equity Modaraba
Jubilee Spin & Weaving
Pilcorp
Premier Insurance
Shakaganj Mills
Shams Textile
Suraj Cotton
**Value of group listed companies: approximately $185 million**

**Iqbal Ali Lakhani** is all too aware that sooner or later the world-wide pressure on smoking and tobacco-related products is going to hit Pakistan with a vengeance. His businesses are already under pressure, due to the widespread illegal trade in smuggled cigarettes between Pakistan and Afghanistan. Thankfully Mr Lakhani has a number of areas into which he can diversify, the most promising of which is probably textiles. His Tritex Cotton Mills, a textile spinning plant with 15,360 spindles, was incorporated in 1987 and listed on the stock exchange in 1991. His cash cow is the Colgate-Palmolive brands he owns for Pakistan, while his Clover Foods company is also potentially fruitful.

*Main Companies*
Century Paper & Board
Clover Foods
Colgate-Palmolive (Pakistan)
Lakson Tobacco
Premier Tobacco
Souvenir Tobacco
Tritex Cotton Mills
**Value of group listed companies: approximately $50 million**

**Mian Mohammad Mansha**'s main interests are in cotton textiles and related products, and by all accounts he is one of the most exciting producers in Pakistan, with his Nishat Mills considered a blue-chip stock. Despite being family-dominated, his companies rely on modern management techniques and are highly professional in all areas of business. They have far-reaching global ambitions, which they may well achieve, particularly in the textile industry. In other sectors, D. G. Khan Cement is one of the largest producers of cement in the north, with an expanded capacity of 5,700 tonnes per day, while Nishat Tek, the group's power company, was one of the first private power plants to be listed on the Karachi Stock Exchange. The company also has a stake in the Muslim Commercial Bank, the largest of the country's privatised banks, with branches throughout Pakistan and abroad.

*Main Companies*
D. G. Khan Cement
First Nishat Modaraba
Genertech
Muslim Commercial Bank
Nishat Chunian
Nishat Fabrics
Nishat Mills
Nishat Tek
Raza Textile Mills
Umer Fabrics
**Value of group listed companies: approximately $270 million**

**M. Asif Saigol** is a manufacturer of cotton yarn as well as of finished cotton products. He was originally part of the Kohinoor Group, which has historically been well placed in the market due to its reputation for quality. Mohib Textile is currently planning to consolidate its businesses into one holding company in order to increase its capital base. Its long-term aim is to become a fully integrated unit, from spinning yarn to producing value-added products.

*Main Companies*
Mohib Exports
Mohib Textile Mills
**Value of group listed companies: approximately $30 million**

**Tariq Saigol**'s companies, now independently run, were once part of what was then known as the Saigol Group. He is the chairman of the All Pakistan Textile Mills Association (APTMA), and as such is the supreme chief of the country's most powerful textile lobbying group. He has been in the textile business for well over a decade and employs modern management techniques to guide his group companies. One of his non-textile companies, Maple Leaf Cement, was acquired from the government as part of its privatisation process. The total capacity of the plant is said to be 546 tonnes, which will be increased to 1,536,500 tonnes in the next year or so.

*Main Companies*
Kohinoor (Gujar Khan) Mills
Kohinoor Sugar Mills
Kohinoor Textile Mills
Kohinoor Weaving
Maple Leaf Cement
**Value of group listed companies: approximately $50 million**

**Naseem Saigol**, also part of the Saigol clan, concentrates his business in a vertically integrated textile processing company, with moves into engineering and the financial services sector. Kohinoor Industries is among the largest textile plants in Pakistan today. The company bank, Union Bank, is a newly established private-sector bank which has ambitions to become an international investment bank through a joint venture. Saigol's other companies are involved in the manufacture of refrigerators, deep freezers, air-conditioners and other small industrial goods. Kohinoor Power, a 24MW captive power plant, feeds the group companies, and a 150MW power plant under the same name is to be established as part of the government's new power policy. This plant will feed the national grid.

*Main Companies*
Union Bank
Union Leasing
*Other Companies*
Azam Textile
Kohinoor Industries
Kohinoor Power
Pak Electron
PEL Appliances
Saritow Spinning
**Value of group listed companies: approximately $130 million**

**Mohammad Saleem**'s main business is textile spinning and the manufacture of cotton yarn. His move into leasing has been a significant and successful departure, and his National Leasing Corporation is now the group's flagship. Most of the company's leasing activities are directed towards capital items such as machinery. Initially Mr Saleem was said by his critics to have received preferential treatment from the government, but nowadays he is certainly far less dependent on political connections. He has the largest of Pakistan's leasing companies, with a total balance sheet in excess of three billion rupees. It is said to have paid-up capital of more than one billion rupees, which is almost double that of its nearest competitor, Orix Leasing, and enjoys about a one-fifth market share. The company is in the early stages of planning joint ventures in equity trading and portfolio management.

*Main Company*
National Leasing Corporation
*Other Companies*
Bhanero Textile Mills
Blessed Textile Mills
Faisal Spinning Mills
**Value of group listed companies: approximately $50 million**

Abdul Shakoor's main business is the manufacture and sale of spun cotton yarn. He comes from a very long line of Pakistani industrialists and is well regarded within the business community. Gulistan Textiles, which was incorporated as a public company in 1966, has a total installed capacity of 65,096 spindles.

*Main Companies*
Gulistan Spinning
Gulistan Textiles
Gulshan Spinning
Paramount Spinning
**Value of group listed companies: approximately $60 million**

Although **Yousuf H. Sherazi**'s main business lies in the financial
services and automotive engineering sectors, he also has in his portfolio an investment bank and a leasing company. His first company,
Muslim Insurance, was set up in 1957. In the mid 1960s he moved
into the auto sector, starting with Atlas Battery, and in August 1994
set up Atlas Honda. The family's auto companies have been manufacturing Honda motorcycles (both 50cc and 125cc) for several years,
and they have recently launched Honda Motorcars in Pakistan, starting with the assembly of units in a plant near Lahore. There are plans
afoot to start manufacturing some parts in other regions in order to
meet the government requirement that a certain number of parts
used in production must be locally made.

On its financial services side, the group has a small investment bank
which is linked to the Bank of Tokyo. Atlas BOT is engaged in investment banking, corporate finance, portfolio management and other
financial advisory services. The Sherazi family are highly regarded
within the business community is Pakistan, and are particularly
admired for the professional management of their group companies.

*Main Companies*
Allwin Engineering
Atlas Battery
Atlas BOT Investment Bank
Atlas BOT Leasing Company
Atlas Honda
Muslim Insurance
**Value of group listed companies: approximately $37 million**

**Abdul Qadir Tawakkal**'s main business is in the manufacture of
wheel rims, and his company is one of a kind in Pakistan, supplying
the entire stock of rims to the country's car manufacturers. The business is growing each day to keep up with increased demand. Mr
Tawakkal also recently bought Naya Daur Motors, a car company,

and plans to reassemble 'Kia' cars and jeeps for the local market.

*Main Companies*
Tawakkal Modaraba
*Other Companies*
Baluchistan Wheels
Hamraz Industries
Tawakkal Garments
Tawakkal Polyester
**Value of group listed companies: approximately $17 million**

A new player, but looking promising, **Rashidullah Yacoob**, unlike most of his peers, is concentrating his energy on the financial services and related sector. The group is said to have professional and well-established management.

*Main Companies*
First Prudential Modaraba
Prudential Discount & Guarantee House
Prudential Investment Bank
Prudential Stocks Fund
Second Prudential Modaraba
Third Prudential Modaraba
*Subsidiary Companies*
Pak I. & C. Leasing
Prime Insurance
**Value of group listed companies: approximately $30 million**

# Bangladesh

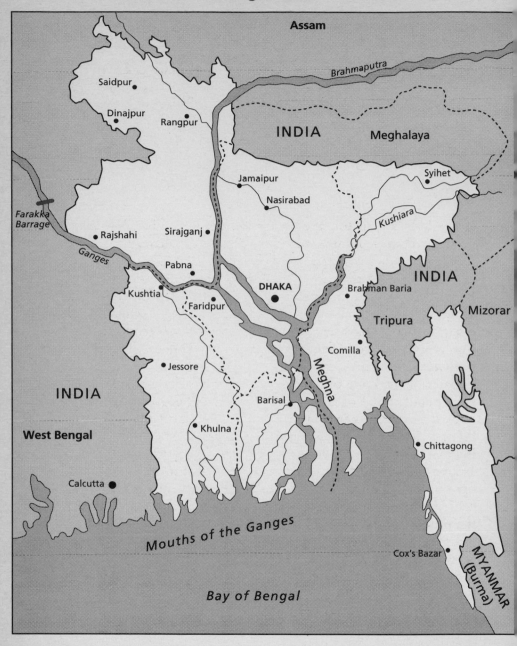

# Chapter 4

# Who's Really Who in Bangladesh

It would be unfair to expect a troubled country like Bangladesh to produce the same number of world-class new maharajahs as India and Pakistan, its sister countries on the subcontinent. That it boasts any at all, with the odds they are up against, is a commercial miracle. Since Bangladesh gained independence from Pakistan in 1971, it has achieved international notoriety for its seemingly endless series of disasters, which have led this strife-torn country to undershoot its five-year plans consistently. Continuous changes of government have not helped matters.

Bangladesh is one of the poorest countries in the world but has a large population – of around 120 million and growing, at a rate said to be 2.5 per cent per annum. The population density is the world's highest, at over 1,940 people per square mile. It is thus not surprising that economic growth has not exactly been rampant, running at around 3.5 per cent, which, though better than many countries in the European Union, is not really enough to deliver a rising standard of living. The single largest problem continues to be malnutrition: the proportion of normally nourished children has risen from about 5.5 per cent ten years ago to only just over 6 per cent today, and acute malnutrition is regularly suffered by one in ten Bangladeshis. It is one of the few countries in the world where the average height of the population is falling, and where women die younger than men. Life expectancy is around fifty-six for men and fifty-four for women, with infant mortality for those between one and four years old at 24 per cent for girls and 14 per cent for boys.

Well over three-quarters of the population of Bangladesh lives in the rural areas, and although this is unlikely to change in the foreseeable future, urbanisation is growing at a rate of about 5 per cent per annum. Official government figures for the adult labour force show that around fifty million people still work in the fields, and child labour, in both town and country, is massively commonplace. Unemployment stands at only 2 per cent, although a great proportion of the population is underemployed, working fewer than twenty hours a week.

The following individuals are Bangladesh's key entrepreneurs, although there are probably millions more struggling to get out of the poverty trap.

**Syed Mansur Elahi** and **M. D. Rahmatullah** became involved in the leather business in 1972 through their role as trading agents for a French company that sold chemicals in Bangladesh. In 1970 they made a bid for Orient Tannery, which was being offered for tender as part of a government decision to privatise tanneries. By 1980 all the company's 'wet blue' production was being exported, mainly to Italy – 'wet blue' being a mechanical and chemical process designed to remove the fat and hair from leather in which chromium sulphate, used to preserve the leather, makes it turn blue. Wet blue leather has a much longer shelf life. While Germany has relocated all its tanneries because of environmental concerns, Bangladesh, sadly, cannot afford the luxury of such considerations, economic survival being uppermost in its mind. In 1982 Apex started producing crust leather, which is a far more capital intensive process. The company achieved a public listing in 1985.

Apex Leathercraft produce 3,000 shoes each day, mainly for the Japanese and Italian markets, and also manufactures leather bags, purses and jackets under international brand names. One of their customers is the Hugo Boss label. In the last year or so, some 60 per cent of the company's exports have gone to mainland China, but they also have clients in South Korea, Thailand, Malaysia and Indonesia, and sell crust leather to Brazil for shoes. Their leather exports total around $170 million per annum, or 8 per cent of the country's exports.

*Main Companies*
Apex Footwear
Apex Tannery
**Value of group listed companies: $18.5 million**

**H. R. Khan** started his ceramics company only just over ten years ago, and it is now producing eighteen million pieces each year and growing at the rate of 20–30 per cent per annum. A man of huge corporate ambition, it is his stated aim to take on one of the world's most significant ceramics leaders, the Japanese firm Noritake. He has an edge in Bangladesh by being able to offer the very best salaries and also, unusually, welfare benefits for his staff. Each employee is also provided with a free umbrella, which in Bangladesh tends to be used more often than not. Mr Khan currently owns two-thirds or so of his country's market share for the industry, but is not dependent on his domestic business: he has a growing client base abroad in a number of very upmarket department stores, including Habitat and Littlewoods in the UK; Galeries Lafayette in France; Country Road in Australia; and Pier One worldwide. The secret of his success has been his willingness to custom-make any order, regardless of time constraints. Key to Mr Khan's expansion are his offices and agents throughout the world, in France, Italy, Holland and the US. He may have to watch out for competition from Eastern Europe and Thailand, but for the moment his healthy revenues and low labour costs remain relatively unchallenged, and his company is a good punt for those brave enough to buy a Bangladeshi stock.

*Main Company*
Monno Ceramic Industries
**Value of group listed companies: approximately $170 million**

The trading company now run by **A. Rahman** started out thirty years ago in the jute business. When that sector was nationalised in 1972, the contacts that the Rahman family retained provided a good base for diversification. The jute mills were returned to the family about ten years ago, but they were in a poor condition, and it is only in the last few years that the company has made a return to the textile business. The Bangladesh Import and Export Company (Beximco) was the first public listed company in Bangladesh, and now has offices in both Britain and the United States. Beximco exports constitute 5 per cent of Bangladeshi national exports. The company deals in marine foods and pharmaceuticals, and also produces bonemeal and imports sugar. The bonemeal is widely used in both Japan and Europe for the manufacture of cellular film and in photosensitive plates for printing.

Beximco tries to launch between three and four new products a year. They have an 11 per cent share of the total pharmaceuticals market and are brand leaders in antibiotics, anti-ulcer drugs, anti-rheumatics, anti-asthmatics, anti-allergenics and vitamins. At one time the Rahman enterprise sold for the German pharmaceutical giant Bayer, but in the 1980s they were forced to develop their own products when importation became too difficult. Bangladesh does offer patent protection but the government requires that the owner of a patent manufacture the medicine locally, within five years of registration.

The company is said to have hidden assets in a shareholding in Padma Textile, a market leader in synthetic yarn which has invested in machinery to produce more upmarket yarn for the export-orientated weaving and knitting mills. Bangladesh still imports some 55 per cent of its total fabric requirements, and 24 per cent of its yarn, so there is nowhere for Padma to go but up.

*Main Company*
Bangladesh Import and Export Company (Beximco)
**Value of group listed company: approximately $5 million**

Chapter 5

# Who's Really Who in the Diaspora

It is said that it is the dream of every person on the subcontinent to become a Non-Resident Indian or an emigré from Pakistan or Bangladesh. There is a gut feeling that somehow things will be better in the West, and once away from home, they often feel much freer to chase success as hard as they can. This is partially why today there are more than fifteen million overseas Indians, who, thanks largely to the legacy of British colonialism, speak, read and write English better than many Westerners. The most cosmopolitan of business people, they face few communications problems in their new homes.

From London to New York, from the Lebanon to Uganda, overseas Indians are a commercial force to be reckoned with. Without their know-how, Silicon Valley in California might well be technically bereft. Men and women from India, Pakistan and Bangladesh make up nearly 5 per cent of the United States' medical staff and an even greater proportion of Britain's national health service. Their impact on the American motel business and the British hotel business frequently goes unremarked. They are a shining example of how immigration may revive a flagging economy in areas which would not otherwise necessarily thrive, for they often release value in a community by finding ways of encouraging a business where others do not even see an opportunity. In the Canary Islands, for example, not exactly the hub of the commercial world, there are said to be some four thousand Sindhis running profitable little businesses.

Many of the new maharajahs have businesses that span the globe, and some operate in countries where British and American companies would fear to tread, such as more terrorist-infested parts of the Middle East. No matter where they may find themselves living, they always consider themselves as transients, not immigrants. They love to be cosmopolitan citizens of the world, and if commercial conditions change, they are happy to move elsewhere.

It is interesting to note that the engine of growth that has acted to accelerate economic development in mainland China – investment from the overseas Chinese – is working similarly on the subcontinent, with Indians, Pakistanis and Bangladeshis who succeed abroad whilst sending money back and developing businesses at home. This has long-term economic benefits for both sides.

Because the subcontinent itself is made up of so many different cultures, religions and languages, it may be argued that its emigrants are better able to cope with the diversity of societies they find themselves living in. At a very early age, Indians are made aware that difference is a challenge, and sometimes an advantage, to be put to good use.

Life in the diaspora, however, does present problems of assimilation and cultural awkwardness. Perhaps surprisingly, there are also problems within the Asian community itself, with certain groups from one part of the subcontinent unable or unwilling to deal with others, even when co-operation would make good commercial sense. Many Westerners forget that there is no such person as an 'Asian'. In India alone one may be a Punjabi, Gujarati, Bengali or Tamil, Muslim, Hindu, Sikh or Christian. People of such diverse cultures and religions should not be lumped together for convenience as many politicians and other businessmen often do.

It is now five decades since large numbers of people from the subcontinent started settling in Britain after Independence. There was another significant influx of Indians in the late 1960s, from East Africa, specifically Uganda and Kenya. In the US, Indian immigration rose nearly 130 per cent during the 1980s, faster than any other group except for those from Vietnam, Cambodia and Laos. The next generation of overseas Indians is likely to achieve even greater success than their parents, as long as the lack of strict Asian morals and the weakening of their once tightly-knit communities does not erode their work ethic. In their desire to be accepted and to succeed, many are losing the qualities of sheer hard work and determination that enabled their mothers and fathers to achieve their commercial dreams.

Almost all Indian emigrés arrived in their new homelands with next to nothing. They formed close communities wherever they found themselves, both for support and in order to create natural markets for goods and services. While this has made their lives economically self-sustaining, it has also frequently been misunderstood, causing resentment and racial prejudice in the wider communities in which they live. Many Westerners fail to see that the closeness within families is a way of ensuring the continuity of an enterprise, brother working with brother, cousin with cousin, trusting each other to pass on the baton. Their Indian dream is only to create a life better than the one left behind. It is worth noting that according to a recent US census, the median annual income of first-generation Indian families is currently the highest of any foreign-born group, at over $50,000.

It would be impossible to enumerate and list all the new maharajahs in the world today. In Asia there are hundreds and thousands of stellar examples, especially in Singapore and Malaysia. In Australia they are legion. Those included here are only the best known.

Like the Chinese, the new maharajahs have a tendency to be unspecific about company structure where the business climate allows. This, deliberately so, makes it very hard indeed to ascertain who exactly owns what where.

## THE UNITED STATES
### Vinod Dham
*Vice President, Intel*
Vinod Dham does not yet run his own major company. Perhaps he is only biding his time, because he most certainly has the capacity to become a significant entrepreneur in his own right. At the moment he has in his hands the fate of the Pentium chip that is revolutionising personal computers. Hundreds of employees work for him, and Intel's research and development capabilities are at his disposal for new technological innovations to be encouraged and trends to be set.

### Umang Gupta
*Computing*
Umang Gupta heads a California software operation that is said to make him worth tens of millions of dollars. He was one of the earliest in the industry to correctly anticipate the profound commercial move away from mainframe to personal computers. He initially graduated from the Indian Institute of Technology, and went on to get an MBA from Kent State University before joining IBM.

## Anil and Sucheta Kapuria
### Computing
Mr and Mrs Kapuria are the proud owners of a $30 million-a-year computer components company based in California's Silicon Valley. Unstoppable, they have recently been funded to the tune of $8 million by Hari Harilela (see p.97) to start up a New Delhi operation to produce computer components for the Indian market.

## Vinod Khosla
### Co-founder of Sun Microsystems
Khosla first read about the creation of the technological giant, Intel, when in his teens, and was inspired. He made his way through college in the US on the strength of scholarships. Now officially retired, even though he is only in his early thirties, he spends his time developing new and interesting projects in the technology sector.

## Sonny Mehta
### Random House
Mehta, who heads three divisions of this publishing house, is said to have fallen in love with English literature when he bought a copy of *Catcher in the Rye* on the streets of New Delhi. His career began in London but he is now based in New York. His success has been enormous, and he has published such literary luminaries as Gabriel García Márquez (*One Hundred Years of Solitude*) and Michael Ondaatje (*The English Patient*).

## Ismail Merchant
### Producer, Merchant-Ivory Films
Given his Indian roots it is not surprising that Merchant makes films with such an English flavour. *Howards End* was produced on a tiny budget, comparatively speaking, of only $8.6 million at a time when the norm was around $30 million. The film brought in some $90 million.

## Ranganath Nayak
### Consultant, Arthur D. Little
Nayak is considered one of the world's greatest authorities when it comes to innovation. His formal education was in mechanical engineering and his doctorate is from the Massachusetts Institute of Technology.

## H. P. Rama
### *The Clarion Hotel, San Francisco*
One of America's new hotel magnates, Mr Rama is developing projects throughout the US, including a 170-room hotel in Orlando, Florida. He frequently works in partnership with another American new maharajah, B. U. Patel.

## Niranjan Shah
### *Engineering and construction*
One of the few new maharajahs in the US to be involved in politics at the highest levels, Mr Shah is a close friend of the Clintons and a serious Democratic fund-raiser. Living today near Chicago, he came originally from a humble village with neither electricity nor running water. His way out was through an engineering scholarship he was awarded by the University of Mississippi.

There are a number of very significant academics in the US who are emigrés from the Indian subcontinent. These include **Professor C. K. Prahalad** at Ann Arbor in Michigan, **Professor Vijay Govindarajan** at the Amos Tuck School of Business at Dartmouth College and **Professor Sam Hari Haran** at the University of Southern California. **Dr Deepak Chopra** has for weeks at a time captured the *New York Times* bestseller list. He has used his knowledge of ayurvedic medicine as the basis of a million-dollar consultancy enterprise and a much watched Public Broadcasting series in the US with fans who include movie actress Demi Moore and others in Hollywood. **Raj Gupta** is another leading Indian intellectual now based in the US and is the head of the major consultancy firm there, McKinsey & Co. Another brilliant academic and innovator is **Amar Bose** of MIT who started the well-known audio products firm Bose Audio, the manufacturers of the critically acclaimed 'Wave' radio.

## THE UNITED KINGDOM
In the UK, twenty of the 500 wealthiest families are Indian. Indians are said to own nearly half of Britain's independent shops. Up to 300 of their 1.5 million number (some 2.7 per cent of the British population) are estimated to be millionaires, whose spending power amounts to more than £5 billion. Yet all too often they go untargeted by mainstream companies.

The richest Indian family in Britain are the Hindujas (see pp.33-

6). According to Gophichand Hinduja, there is now no business, other than alcohol and meat, that they would not be in if the income warranted it. They continue to operate mostly out of Europe, specifically London and Geneva, and have plans for major investments in telecommunications, transportation, power generation and petroleum all over the world.

### Ashraf Adamjee
*Steel and chemicals*
Part of the prominent Pakistani Adamjee family (see p.66), Ashraf graduated from Harvard with an MBA after being educated at Millfield School in Britain. He now trades with India in chemical products and steel, working together with his daughter, Manizeh. Ashraf is thought to have personal wealth in the region of £20 million.

### Shami and Nizam Ahmed
*The Legendary Joe Bloggs Jean Co.*
Thought to be worth something in the region of £25 million Shami Ahmed, who lives in Cheshire, has built up a fashion empire that is the envy of all his fellow Mancunians. It was only thirty years ago that his father, Nizam, left Pakistan to work on a market stall. Within the last five years, Shami Ahmed produced the most expensive trousers the world has ever seen: diamond-encrusted jeans which cost more than £100,000. He also has a property business with £20 million of assets.

### Yaqub Ali
*Cash and carry*
Also from Pakistan, Mr Ali, who started out in the UK as a door-to-door salesman, now owns Europe's largest wholesale warehouse – in the infamous Gorbals area of Glasgow. With personal wealth of around £20 million, he was assiduously wooed by former prime minister Margaret Thatcher, for whom he often held fund-raising dinners in Scotland.

### Prem Anand
*Marvel Fair*
Said to be worth around £15 million, Mr Anand trades in a very unusual sector: militaria and uniforms. Based in Wembley, in north-

west London, he has been in Britain for over three decades, after an earlier period in West Africa.

## Suhail Aziz
### Brettonwood Management Consultants
Mr Aziz, a management consultant, is one of the most successful of the UK-based Bangladeshi new maharajahs.

## Raj Kumar and Apurv Bagri
### Metdist and Minmetco
A former filing clerk in Calcutta, commodity dealer Raj Kumar Bagri is today worth something in the region of £70 million. He and his son, Apurv, are among the City's most formidable brokers, and he is also vice chairman of the London Metals Exchange. The pair are currently investing around $400 million in a combined copper smelter and sulphuric acid refinery in western India.

## Bhushan Bharadwaj
### The Sunflower Group
Originally from the Punjab, Bhushan Bharadwaj started his multi-million-pound textile business twenty-five years ago, when he arrived in Britain from Kenya. Based in Harrow, in north-west London, today his empire reaches as far as Africa.

## Gulshen Bhatia
### The Great Western Hotel
An emigrant from Tanzania to Britain, Mrs Bhatia built her £35 million hotel empire on a portfolio which includes the Great Western Hotel at Paddington Station. Now in her sixties, she came to the UK as a widow, turning to business as a means of survival for her family.

## Ratilal Chandaria and brothers
### Comcraft
The Chandarias, much like the Hindujas, are hugely secretive about their business. We do know, however, that their steel, chemicals and plastics empire has operations in some forty countries. They have a charitable foundation based in Switzerland, and their personal wealth is estimated to be something in the region of £50 million.

### Damodar Chanrai and brothers
*The J. T. Chanrai Group*
Mr Chanrai and his family are thought to be worth around £60 million. Their main business is steel and textiles, but other family members are also involved with hotels and fashion. Their empire spans several countries, including some in Africa and Asia.

### Satish, Rushmie and Jay Chatwani
*Hotels*
The Chatwani brothers, all highly qualified accountants, built their £30 million fortune by identifying underpriced middle-ranking hotels, which they improved and sold on to upgrade their portfolio. They originally came to Britain from Uganda.

### Murli and Suresh Chellaram
### Pishu and Hari Chellaram
### Lokumal, Sham and Lal Chellaram
*Trading*
The wealth of the Chellarams is thought to be around £30 million. They are a distinguished Sindhi trading family, with other involvements in manufacturing and shipping. They have significant business operations in Nigeria.

### Ramesh Dewan
*Trans-Brittania Properties*
Based in north London and worth at least £20 million, Mr Dewan is a director of over forty companies, spanning the property and publishing worlds. The origins of his success with Trans-Brittania lie in construction.

### Gurdip Singh Gujral
*Jasko India Ltd.*
Arriving in Britain thirty years ago, Gurdip Gujral worked for a time in a factory to make ends meet. Today he drives a Rolls Royce, and is known to be highly philanthropic, donating large amounts to charity. A London-based clothing importer, Mr Gujral is thought to be worth at least £10 million. His main import markets are India, Pakistan, Thailand and Afghanistan.

## Om Prakash Gulati
*Welcome Travel*
Thirty years ago, Om and his younger brother Vijay, came to Britain and set up a discount travel business in Harrow, where they now live. At that time this was a new trend, and the brothers blossomed, particularly in catering to the market of Indians returning home to see relatives. The Gulatis are said today to be worth over £10 million. Welcome Travel is now the Air India general sales agent in Britain.

## Pravin, Bibhaker, Bhjarat and Mitesh Jitania
*Lornamead beauty products*
Today worth some £15 million, the four Jitania brothers came to Britain from Uganda in the 1970s. They now own an ethnically-targeted cosmetics house which enjoys healthy exports to the USA, Europe and Africa, and their products are widely available through Boots and other chemists' shops.

## Nurdin and Nick Jivrai
*Buckingham International Group*
Probably worth around £50 million through their property interests in Britain and Portugal, these emigrés arrived in London from Tanzania in the early 1970s.

## Bimal, Ramesh and Samesh Kumar
*Fashion and textiles*
Today worth more than £20 million, the Kumar brothers came to Britain from India in the 1960s, when their father ran a market stall in Manchester. They are all graduates of Salford University and instead of selling fruit are dealing in an annual turnover of around £4 million worth of clothing and accessories.

## Gula and Partap Lalvani
*Electronics*
Born in Karachi and brought up in Bombay, the Lalvanis arrived in the north of England in their late teens, and started out in the jewellery business before moving on to buying cheap electronic goods from Korea and Hong Kong. Today they are consumer electronic giants, based in Leeds and worth some £25 million. Their flagship company is Dialatron, one of the UK's best-known vendors of mobile phones.

### Lakhi Liyanage
*The Castel Group*

Mr Liyanage, a Sri Lankan-born accountant, has a large commercial and residential property portfolio and is chairman of the computer-industry-based Castel Group. Amongst other interests, they also manufacture wood products, fire doors and windows.

### Manubhai, Pratap, Surendra and Mayur Madhvani
*Sugar, glass, steel and electronics*

The Madhvanis are said to have once controlled about 10 per cent of Uganda's GDP before Idi Amin appropriated their businesses in 1972. Today Manubhai has been given back his sugar mill, and the Ugandan government has even taken a one-third stake. The brothers' worldwide operations has offices throughout the Middle East and Africa as well as in London, and they are today worth some £185 million.

### Vijay Mallya
*Brewing*

Worth at least £80 million, Vijay (see pp.54–5) succeeded his father in the family business, the UB Group, just over ten years ago. He is now based in Surrey, from where he runs the newly renamed Inn Business Group, although he makes frequent forays back to India. He has a fine collection of old cars and is said to love horse-racing.

### Mahesh Kumar
*Stockbroker*

Mr Kumar is currently employed by City brokers Dean Witter, and has started a networking body for Asian professionals, the Asian City Club.

### Hasso Melwani
*The G. Daulatram Group*

Based in London's St John's Wood, Mr Melwani's £15 million fortune is based on textiles. He also works with his close relative, Ram, in other areas of trading, dealing extensively with a number of African countries.

### Tariq Mohammed and Tahir Mohsan
*Time Computers UK Ltd.*

These brothers run their Time Computers company out of Burnley,

Lancashire, and are considered to be worth something in the region of £40 million. Tahir left school at sixteen to set up a mail-order business, and has never looked back.

## Nurdin Nanji
*The Wayeach Consultancy*
Born in Tanzania, Mr Nanji has a £55 million fortune based on property, commodities and shipping. Now living in Highgate, he has major operations in both London and the UAE, and works closely with both his sons and his brothers.

## G. K. Noon
*Frozen foods*
It is difficult to establish the extent and value of Mr Noon's commercial empire, but we do know that he is one of the largest suppliers of frozen Indian dishes to supermarkets in Britain.

## C. B. Patel
*Asian business publisher*
Mr Patel has developed a niche market for his publications, which cater to the growing interest in doing business with countries in the Asian–Pacific region.

## Charles Patel
*Vapgate Ltd.*
With over 300 shops to his name, Mr Patel has turned the corner newsagent into a significant retailing space. Not only do they stay open long hours, they also sell all manner of useful food items, and, of course, lottery tickets. Based in north London, he came to Britain from Fiji forty years ago, and is now worth more than £20 million.

## Dadu Patel
*Chemist's shops and property*
A barrister by profession, Dadu Patel came to Britain from Kenya to read for the bar at Lincoln's Inn. Apart from a west London shopping complex, a chain of chemist's shops and a cash and carry, he now has interests in a 5-star hotel in London and a vast industrial complex near Heathrow, and is worth over £20 million.

### Girish Patel
*Manila Commodities*

Girish Patel came to London only in the 1970s. It was his grandfather who started the family business, Manila Commodities, in 1932, in Penang, Malaysia. Today it is one of the world's largest commodity traders, dealing in palm oil, cocoa, rubber and tin, and is worth around £50 million.

### Naresh, Mahesh and Jitu Patel
*Europa food shops*

Naresh Patel's Europa chain of upmarket London food shops has made him worth well over £18 million. Born in Kenya, he took over an existing food group, and together with his brother, transformed the style and trading hours of local shopping.

### Pradyuman Rajeshwar Patel
*Letap Pharmaceuticals and Regent Laboratories*

Today worth around £30 million, Mr Patel came to the UK from Uganda, and set up his empire in pharmaceuticals. He also has substantial property and aviation interests, and owns a number of licensed taxi operations.

### Swraj Paul
*Caparo*

Swraj Paul, who was recently made a Life Peer in Britain, and his Harrow-educated sons, Ambar and Akash, are the most established of Britain's resident Indians. The group is thought to be worth about £500 million. Mr Paul brought his family to Britain in the 1960s, seeking a cure for his daughter's leukaemia. Sadly she was not to survive. Caparo, predominantly in the business of steel tube manufacturing, was founded about thirty years ago when Mr Paul bought a steel company which today employs over 5,000 people. Not long ago the family set up a steel plant in north-eastern India which Mr Paul plans to dedicate to his daughter. In a joint venture with the Indian government, Caparo's equity contribution to the $2 billion project is thought to be about $90 million. In 1995, the family took over a redundant steel mill in Pennsylvania.

## Anwar Pervez
### Bestway Cash and Carry
A fiercely proud Muslim, Mr Pervez is said to be 'Britain's Cash and Carry King', even though he only started the company twenty years ago. He also operates the Bestway Foundation, which gives generously to the community.

## Rajan Pillai
### Cashews and food
One of Pillai's most lucrative companies was the subject of a successful takeover bid by R J Nabisco which partially contributed to Mr Pillai's estimated wealth of around £20 million. Only in his early forties and living in London, Mr Pillai conducts his business throughout the world but is said to be concentrating on expanding more into Asia.

## Nat Puri
### Milton Medes
Nat Puri came to Britain from the Punjab thirty years ago, working as an engineer in Nottingham until he formed his own company. He has tried to target a number of prominent British companies, including Rover and what were the British Builders' Shipyards in Sunderland. He also has a stake in Delaney, a quoted kitchen and bathroom manufacturer, and is worth around £125 million.

## Rasik and Anant Rabheru
### The Park Hotels Group
The Rabheru family, hugely successful in the hotel industry, are now thought to be worth around £150 million, yet they came to Britain from Tanzania only just over twenty-five years ago. Their 1,500-room chain now extends from Brighton to Cheltenham and features some prime properties in central London.

## Amritlal and Mansukh Radia
### The Marn Group
The Radia brothers, members of the Hindu Gujarati Lohana sect, arrived in Britain from Uganda in the 1970s. Early on in the life of their car dealership, they won for themselves the highly lucrative Fiat contract. They also have extensive property interests, and are worth over £10 million.

## Anil Ruia
### The Bombay Trading Company
Anil Ruia's father, Govindji, started the Bombay Trading Company (Botraco) on his arrival in London from India. Anil is now based in Manchester and is worth some £10 million from general trading and textile interests. He also has flourishing tea estates in India.

## Salman Rushdie
### Writer
A new maharajah of the less pecunious kind, the profusely talented Mr Rushdie must be included here for his somewhat notorious stature as an emigré from the subcontinent. Born in Bombay, he is still hiding in Britain under an Iranian death sentence because of alleged blasphemy in his novel The Satanic Verses.

## Roy Sandhu
### Textiles
Mr Sandhu left Delhi just over thirty years ago and set up his textiles company in the poorest part of the East End of London. Though he started out very modestly, with his Roy Fashions, he is now worth well over £20 million. He also has interests in the food business, and is a major landlord in the Docklands area of London.

## Anant Shah
### The Meghraj Bank
Anant Shah, a banker and venture capitalist, was born in Kenya and came to England to be educated. After finishing school at Haberdashers' Aske's in Elstree, he went on to the London School of Economics, to prepare himself to take over the Meghraj Bank, started by his father.

## Arun, Nitin and Milan Shah
### The Pepe Group
Nitin Shah came to Britain from Kenya less than thirty years ago and got into the clothing business. The family's £30 million empire was founded on a modest but highly successful boutique in the King's Road, Chelsea, which grew to encompass wholesale commercial activities. The company was floated on the London Stock Exchange just over ten years ago.

## Lakshmi Shivdasani
### Brewing and aluminium

Lakshmi Shivdasani is a new maharajah with more than £100 million in assets. She has interests in brewing, food and provisions and aluminium, and her empire, which she manages together with her children, reaches into India and Nigeria as well as the UK.

## Jasminder Singh
### The Edwardian Hotel Group

Today worth at least £90 million, Mr Singh is perhaps best known for his ownership of the Edwardian Hotel Group, which has in its portfolio some of the best hotels in central London. He was trained as a chartered accountant and came to Britain from Kenya just over thirty-five years ago.

## Tom Singh
### New Look fashions

Worth around £115 million, Tom Singh came to Britain from the Punjab to live in Dorset, where his father owned a drapery shop. He has in fact sold New Look, for £170 million, and is actively involved in a number of other ventures.

## Taherbhai Sutterwalla
### T. R. Sutterwall & Sons

Based in the import and export sector, this food business, which is said to be worth something in the region of £18 million, was started when Mr Sutterwalla left Bombay for Britain over four decades ago. At that time there were very few ethnic foods available in the UK, a state of affairs which the Sutterwallas have done their best to remedy.

## Ashok Tandon
### Million Dollar Homes

A property developer worth at least £10 million, Mr Tandon came to Britain from East Africa and now lives in London. His extravagant corporate projects have included the 'Summer Palace', a £12 million house in Hampstead.

## Rashid Tayub
### The Crown Crest Cash & Carry

Rashid Tayub came to Britain from Malawi in 1976. He started out with a small shop in Huddersfield and today runs his £15 million cash-and-carry operation from Nottingham.

### Rashmi Thakrar
*Tilda Rice Ltd.*
A glowing success story to the tune of at least £20 million, the Thakrar family arrived in Britain in 1972 from Uganda, having been thrown out by Idi Amin. They may rightfully claim to dominate over half of Britain's trade in rice.

### Vinod Vadera
*Property*
Born in Uganda, Vinod Vadera also came to Britain in 1972. He owns businesses in Britain, Canada and India, and is worth about £20 million.

### Charanjit and Satinder Vohra
*Hotels*
Brothers Charanjit and Satinder, who were born in Kenya, are worth nearly £80 million through their ownership of one of London's largest hotel chains. Satinder's nephew, Jasminder Singh, is also a major owner of London hotel properties.

### Chatru Wadhwani
*Textile mills*
Mr Wadhwani, a Sindhi, has over £20 million in assets. He is based in Britain, with a home in London's Regent's Park, and owns textile mills in Nigeria.

## THE REST OF THE WORLD
In Hong Kong, businessmen from the subcontinent account for one-tenth of the colony's exports, even though they comprise less than 1 per cent of the population. The most significant of these are the Harilela family who own property and hotels across Asia. Brothers Hari, Bob and Gary and others not only work side by side, but their six families, plus that of a married sister, also live together in an enormous mansion in Kowloon. The household is so large that it employs thirty-five maids, three chefs and a former hotel manager. The family's numerous companies include Harilela's Properties & Investment Ltd., Hotel Holdings Ltd., Ashoka Investment Ltd.,

Kowloon Estates Investment Ltd. and Gaylord Hotels & Restaurants Ltd.

Other Hong Kong new maharajahs include: large numbers of the Ruttonjee family; Amitabha Chowdury, owner of Asian Financial Publications Ltd.; Gopaldas B. Bahbubani; Gulab B. Thadani; Gopalakrishnan Piliai; members of the Shroff family; Mahabir Mohindar, the lively owner of Communications Management Ltd., which includes in its stable no less a publication than the *Hong Kong Tatler*; and Rana Talwar, the head of Citibank's consumer banking division in Asia.

There is a very large community of Indians and others from the subcontinent throughout Asia. Significant amongst these are **Lakshmi Mittal** of Ispat who is based in Jakarta and **Murli Kewalram Chanrai** of the eponymous US billion-dollar group based in Singapore with business interests throughout Asia and Africa. His company also has a textile manufacturing operation in the Philippines, Kewalram Philippines. Chanrai was chairman of the first Global Indian Entrepreneurs Conference held in 1996 in Singapore.

Also particularly notable in southeast Asia are **Robin Wasvani**, a member of the family that owns the only lens manufacturing facility in the Philippines; the co-ordinator of the Philippines Economic Zone at Bandung, **Nam Prasad** and **Hiro Asandas**, president of a major linen and children's wear export house called New Creation Manufacturing. **Nari Genomal** runs V Lilaram, the company that holds the regional licence for the internationally renowned 'Jockey' brand of briefs. **Vashi Badlani** is a textile exporter who is now investing back in India and also **John Daswani** whose J D Textile Industries is a major garment manufacturer. **Ferdinand Nanki Hiranand** owns the string of 'Jollibee' fast food outlets whose hamburgers outsell McDonalds in the Philippines. Jollibee also now sells in Guam, Brunei, Dubai and Los Angeles. Hiranand is keen to open Jollibee fast food outlets in a number of Indian cities.

There are also 600,000 Indians in Saudi Arabia, and 35,000 in Germany. There are no limits to where the new maharajahs will go – quite literally, it seems, to the ends of the earth: Bezal Jesudason, a native of sultry Madras, runs a seven-room inn in Resolute Bay, Canada, for travellers on their way to the North Pole, 1,050 miles away. He lives happily with a mean temperature of minus 60 degrees Fahrenheit, and his only comment is: 'You just have to dress right.'

# Chapter 6

# The Home Turf:
# Industrial Sectors

This is not a comprehensive attempt to analyse and discuss all of the subcontinent's industrial sectors, but is intended as a rough guide to those areas in which the new maharajahs take their most active roles.

ALUMINIUM
Aluminium is the mainstay and *sine qua non* of vehicle production and most types of industrial manufacturing. In 1992, as part of the general trend towards liberalisation, the Indian government reduced the heavy import duties that protected domestic manufacturers of aluminium, with the effect that Indian producers were no longer marginalised from global trends.

India's per capita consumption of aluminium is only 1kg against a global average of 30kg. However, strong industrial production and burgeoning demand for cars should mean that output will grow at around 7 per cent over the next few years. With the foreign investment boom that India has been enjoying, infrastructure industries have been going through a growth period, and there has been an increase in production facilities for the electronics sector. It is therefore not surprising that the new maharajahs in this sector are likely to continue to go from strength to strength. Their long-term profitability is assured, even though, apart from the low-cost producers, short-term profits may be somewhat squeezed. Adding to their security is the knowledge that supply in India continues to be unable to keep up with demand, so they can keep their prices high and boost earnings and income. Crucial to aluminium production is the plentiful supply of inexpensive bauxite and an abundance of power. In India power is always a problem, so those companies situated in states fortunate enough to have reliable generation have a significant advantage. Those who can achieve self-sufficiency, as some companies do, are able to maintain a commanding position in the industry.

The largest aluminium producer in the country is the National Aluminium Company (NALCO), which, along with another significant manufcturer, the Bharat Aluminium Company, is government-owned. Two other major companies – Hindalco and the Indian Aluminium Company (INDAL) – are in the hands of the private sector. INDAL has to rely to some extent on its power supply from the state, and is therefore more vulnerable than NALCO.

Some companies take production further down the chain, producing not just aluminium but also derivative products such as extruders and rollers. Hindalco Industries Ltd., 21.1 per cent owned by the Birla family through the Aditya Birla company, is India's largest private-sector producer of both primary aluminium and aluminium products, accounting for about 40 per cent of the country's production. The company is substantially integrated vertically, from bauxite mining to power generation, and also meets its chemical requirements from within the group.

## AUTOMOBILES AND TRANSPORTATION

The automobile industry in India, and throughout the subcontinent in general, is rapidly changing. The big wheels amongst the new maharajahs include the Anand family group; the Munjals, through Hero Cycles, the world's largest bicycle manufacturer; and the Bajaj family, who own and run the fourth-largest two-wheeler company in the world and control nearly half of the Indian market. Bajaj Auto seems to be concentrating on new product lines, and is spending heavily to expand production capacity and allow for economies of scale, and to improve cost competitiveness. The Birlas, who own Hindustan Motors, General Motors' joint venture partner in India, are prominent in the sector, as also are the Firodia family, who make components as well as their famous Luna, Spark and Safari scooters and Honda cars; the Kalyani steel family, who manufacture automotive axles and hi-tech hydraulic brakes together with Japan's NAPCO; and, of course, the Tatas, who in many ways are the fathers of Indian automotive success, having entered the strategic and infrastructure sectors of the business back in 1945, just when the industry was being set up. Mahindra & Mahindra have enjoyed growing profits but have had troubles with unions, including a five-month lockout at one production plant and a go-slow at another, which caused a downturn in the sales of their utility vehicles.

In 1987, the Hinduja brothers, whose business interests had until then been strictly confined to film-making, bought a British-held controlling stake in Ashok Leyland, a publicly quoted bus- and lorry-maker. It is said that the brothers' political connections must have been most useful in swatting away any competition for the group. The Hindujas through Ashok Leyland have sales estimated at $400 million a year and a 25–30 per cent share of India's bus and lorry market, and they would like to expand to make three-wheeled vehicles, tractors and components. They have also been discussing for some time a tie-up with a Japanese company, which should make them one of India's biggest car-makers.

Commercial vehicle demand is heavily geared to economic activity. Strong industrial growth backed by increasing investment in infrastructure will drive demand up by 20-25 per cent over the next two years. Railway capacity has been stagnating because of a cut in budgetary support, with the result that a great deal more is being transported by road, and the sharp increase in the country's international trade has also played its part, since the major sea ports are serviced mainly by roads.

There seems to be a trend towards the use of specialised, so-called niche vehicles, both light and heavy. The launch by Ashok Leyland and Telco of seven- and nine-tonne cargo vehicles fitted with the latest Iveco engines is an illustration of this. Rising interest rates have not halted demand, because high freight rates have made these trucks more economically viable for the operators. Tight liquidity is a concern, though, as the major truck financing companies such as Sundaram Finance ease the problem only temporarily.

## BANKS AND FINANCIAL INSTITUTIONS

Amongst those who have recently moved into the financial sector are the Birla Group, with Birla Global Finance Ltd.; Bharat Ram, through his CDM Ltd.; the Ruias, with India Securities Ltd.; and the ubiquitous Hindujas. Khodadad Farmanfarmian, the Hindujas' chief financial adviser in London, is exploring how best they should extend their involvement in the sector. There was talk of Mr Mittal, who seems to want to be all things to all people, setting up a financial services company, as part of his grand design to become a truly multinational company, while GESCO, the Sheth family's shipping company, has entered investment banking, equity trading and other financial services through its company Prime Securities Ltd. The ever-enterprising Ambanis have set up Reliance Capital Ltd. and have further plans in the financial sector to complement their existing fund management group, securities trading operation, commercial bank and custodial services division. Less directly involved are those new maharajahs in the technology and information service areas, who pay very close attention to developments in the financial sector because it is such a huge market for their wares. Infosys, for example, is well aware that companies with financial interests are among the largest users of computerisation.

For some time now, the demand in India for credit has been strong, but the supply of funds is insufficient. This is largely because of a tight monetary policy to curb inflation, and because the last government continually accessed the markets to fund the deficit. As a result, interest rates rose, which in turn dampened profitability because the banks retain a big chunk of government securities as assets. In addition to an investment portfolio with maturities of different durations, many of the old private banks have securities with very low coupon rates, and as a result most of them will have to take a write-off. Many of the new private banks run by new maharajahs have been in operation for less than a couple of years, and the relatively small size of their investment portfolio will limit the absolute amount of depreciation. There could be plenty of room for growth with joint ventures in the securities sector.

## CEMENT

The cement sector is highly geared to economic growth. This is because it caters to core sectors but is capital intensive in nature and characterised by cyclical ups and downs. As investment costs have risen, most producers are moving towards large-capacity production, so that the investment cost per tonne is lower, with higher economies of scale. Although the industry faces increasing infrastructural problems, in the form of rising wages, inadequate coal supplies and frequent power cuts, growth in demand averages 8 per cent per annum. The geographical location of the producer is vital, with growth seeming to be strongest in the western part of the country and weakest in the eastern. The current installed production capacity in India is about 91 million tonnes per annum, with more than 90 per cent of this in the private sector. Nevertheless, the new maharajahs have to cope with extensive government intervention, since nearly half of the total input costs come from sectors that are still heavily under central or state government control. The government is also the industry's largest customer, accounting for nearly 15–20 per cent of total sales.

One of the key inputs for the industry is electricity, which is supplied by state electricity boards. The supply is unreliable, with frequent ad hoc and sometimes unexpected price rises. Most of the major cement-producing states – such as Rajasthan, Madhya Pradesh and Andhra Pradesh – experience regular power cuts which can cause quite substantial loss of production. As a result, big companies like ACC and Madras Cements rely on captive power. Those companies based in the south have concentrated on setting up power-generating windmills. Companies like Madras Cement and Gujarat Ambuja, whose electricity consumption is significantly lower than many others, have a distinct cost advantage.

## COMPUTERS, SOFTWARE AND CONSUMER ELECTRONICS

The figures for projected growth in India in consumer electronics alone show that a 30 per cent annual growth is expected for the next five years at least. A number of major international companies are expected to enter the market, however, thereby inevitably cutting the profits of the new maharajahs. In the IT sector, India's largest software export house is owned by the Tata Group. F. C. Kohli, deputy chairman of Tata Consultancy Services (TCS), and considered to be 'the father of Indian information technology', has watched, with sometimes ill-concealed wrath, as the Indian government has slowed or halted technological advances. TCS are concentrating their energies on existing computer businesses, and are planning to consolidate by entering new areas of expertise which will, they hope, make them increasingly globally competitive. Like so many of India's industrial sectors, the software industry was liberalised by Narasimha Rao after July 1991. Up until that time, potential had been limited by the government's command-and-control economic policy, with its endless regulations, tariffs and import bans.

Bangalore is India's own Silicon Valley. Foreign multinationals such as IBM, Texas Instruments, Digital Equipment Corporation, Hewlett Packard, Motorola and 3M have set up local operations, and the city is putting the finishing touches to a $150 million science park which is home to a number of India's own high-tech high-fliers, such as Infosys and Satyam Computers. The former, which enjoys annual international sales of $10 million and a market capitalisation of $70 million, was set up back in 1981 by a group of seven software professionals. The five who remain have developed expertise in different functions and work as a close-knit team under the leadership of chairman and MD Narayana Murthy. The middle management, which copes with day-to-day operations, is also strong and experienced. Infosys has marketing offices in Boston and San Francisco, and its major clients include General Electric, J. P. Morgan, Nestlé, AT&T, Reebok, Salomon S.A. of France, Holiday Inn, Nordstrom, NYNEX, Apple and Hitachi.

Thanks to a satellite link built by the government, Infosys's terminals are hooked to a network that keeps them in contact with their customers in America and Europe. The company employs 600 high-quality software engineers, and they are able to choose the best from the top engineering schools. Infosys is the first Indian software company to formalise the concept of employee stock options, and when these are exercised in 1999, employee ownership of the company will rise to 10 per cent.

Satyam Computers is also a professionally managed software company, and is one of the few in India to have obtained the ISO9000 and the higher-level TickIT certifications. Its client list comprises medium-size Fortune 500 companies, half a dozen of whom have the potential to provide the company with $3–4 million worth of business every year. Satyam was incorporated in 1987 as a 100 per cent export-orientated unit to provide software development and consultancy services to large corporations. The owners, Ramalinga and Rama Raju, have considerable business experience, as well as business management degrees, while their cousin Srini Raju, the real force behind the company's strategy and day-to-day management, has a Masters degree in science and worked in the US computer software industry before joining the family business.

Wipro Infotech is the software subsidiary of Wipro, a family-owned trading group which was once known best for its vegetable oils but which the younger generation of the family is trying to focus on technology. Over 80 per cent of Wipro Infotech's sales of $80 million comes from exports to high-tech American clients such as AT&T, Intel and Sun Microsystems.

There are now said to be over 550 Indian software companies in the country. Although most of these are small-scale in nature, the top twenty account for more than 63 per cent of the country's total exports. Indian software exports are dominated by contract programming (60 per cent), followed by turnkey contracts (32 per cent) and products and systems integration (8 per cent), but the country's presence in the product segment is negligible, with exports of just $6 million out of a global market of $440 billion. To make amends, Satyam has a joint venture with Dunn & Bradstreet, the world's biggest database provider, and Infosys developed a distribution system in a tie-up with Reebok France which was later sold as a product.

Software exports have grown to more than thirty times their previous size in the last eight years. Nowadays 58 per cent goes to the USA, 20 per cent to Europe, 6 per cent to south-east Asia, 4 per cent to west Asia, 3 per cent to Japan, 3 per cent to Australia and New Zealand and 6 per cent to the rest of the world. The top ten exporters by turnover are Tata Consultancy Services, Tata Unisys, Pentafour Software, Silverline, Infosys Technology, Digital Equipment India, Fujitsu ICIM, Square D Software, Patni Comp and NIIT. The top ten domestic software firms by turnover are Tata Consultancy Services, CMC, Onward Novell Software India, Oracle Software India, Tata Unisys, Sonata Software, PCL, NIIT, Siemens and Mastek.

According to a World Bank report on the Indian software industry, the country's 'foreign opportunity' is around 12 per cent, with foreign opportunity measured by taking a composite of international demand for software and services, the competition that India faces from other software-exporting countries, and strategies adopted by the country to secure an increased global market share. The advantage that India has in manpower availability is increasing its ranking. Given that the global software market is expected to increase to around $200 billion a year within five years, the future rate of growth in India's software sector may well make it the fastest-growing segment in the country's electronic industry. Few doubt that India has the capability to meet the intellectual challenge of software writing, for the country has one of the largest talent pools in the world, and a solid educational system. What they need now is the spirit of risk to take the next step to fullscale product development.

## FERTILISERS

Agriculture is the mainstay of the Indian economy, and even with burgeoning industry and the growth of other key sectors, agriculture-related output still accounts for nearly one-third of India's GDP. Both nitrogenous (urea) and phosphatic fertilisers play a crucial role in improving crop yields and form an integral part of modern farming. Successive cropping depletes the main soil nutrients, nitrogen, phosphorus and potassium, which have to be replaced. Fertilisers are divided, broadly speaking, into simple and complex types, the former replenishing just the one key nutrient, the latter many. Urea, a straight nitrogenous fertiliser, meets over 80 per cent of the total nitrogen nutrient requirement, and di-ammonium phosphate meets 50 per cent of the phosphatic requirement. The balance is made up by single super phosphate and other complex fertilisers.

It is economically imperative for India that the fertiliser sector is as successful as it can possibly be. One key area is the production of urea, which was decontrolled in a piecemeal fashion, beginning with the deregulation of some phosphatic fertilisers in 1992. As India still faces a shortfall in the supply of the basic feed stocks necessary for urea production, it is unlikely that the producers will be able to improve their positioning in global production. The availability of natural gas, the main feed stock for urea, is a particular concern. Many major fertiliser corporates are diversifying away to cope with their problems in this sector: Indo Gulf Fertilisers is moving into copper smelting and paper, SPIC into pharmaceuticals and LPG and Nagarjuna Fertilisers into steel, while other companies such as Zuari (the Birla Group), SPIC and Chambal Fertilisers are planning urea plants in countries like Syria and the UAE which have assured and cheap availability of natural gas.

## HOTELS

There is tremendous potential for India to attract foreign visitors, but due to poor promotion, inadequate infrastructural facilities, bad flight connections and the lack of proper coordination between the tour operators and the hotels, this has remained largely untapped. While Hong Kong, for instance, attracts five million tourists a year, India has only two million visitors. With strong entry barriers, high capital costs, long gestation periods and difficulties in procuring land, those already in the hotel business in the cities cannot fail to continue to do very well.

Tourism in India – and as a corollary hotel occupancy – has until recently always been seasonal, with April to September being the most slack time. Most foreign tourists visit India between October and March, so that is the peak season for the country's hotel industry. Occupancy rates, which are about 40–50 per cent during the slack season, can go as high as 90–100 per cent at peak times. The boom in the luxury hotel sector has been led by a sharp increase in the number of business travellers, both foreign and domestic, rushing around India to make lucrative deals. This increase has also changed the traditional seasonality, which in turn has led to a jump in average room and occupancy rates. For those involved, like the Tatas, the Oberois and the Birlas, the large proportion of foreign exchange earnings acts as a very useful hedge against a depreciation of the rupee.

The hotel industry in India has been given many government incentives, primarily tax breaks. Half of the foreign exchange earned by government-approved hotels is exempt from tax, and if the other half in invested in a tourism-related enterprise, then that too is tax-free. The Department of Tourism has classified the country's hotels with a star rating of 1 to 5, and 5-star deluxe. There is also a heritage hotel category, in which are included old palaces or castles that have been converted. Most investment has gone into the 5-star hotels, which account for some 33 per cent of the total number of rooms. About 76 per cent of the total number of 5-star rooms are concentrated in Bombay and Delhi.

In India, building can take a great deal of time, and a 200-room 5-star hotel might not be completed for two or three years. Land is a major constraint for many hotel companies wanting to expand their operations: in the cities it is extremely expensive, and in many areas – such as Bombay's business district or tourist spots like Agra – is very hard to come by. To increase occupancy rates, hotels will typically offer discounts on the published tariffs. The size of these varies according to the client, and the location, size and quality of the hotel.

## MEDIA AND ENTERTAINMENT
There is no doubting the profound effect that liberalisation has had for the new maharajahs involved in the media and entertainment. The growth in consumption in the television industry will only continue with a rise in consumer spending. Artificial barriers to entry have been considerably reduced, and increased investment and the proliferation of technology are making for a rosy future. While

progress will be much slower than many other countries in Asia, entertainment retail and out-of-home entertainment facilities, especially cinemas, are developing throughout the subcontinent. The persistent power problems will of course create problems along the way.

By the year 2000, television advertising, particularly on cable and satellite, will surge as more homes buy sets. It is estimated that 60 per cent of programmes will be in Hindi and 10 per cent in English, while some 20 per cent will come from the Asian-Pacific region. One of the most interesting of the television companies, Zee, is destined to reach high levels of viewership and is already considered to be a company setting industry standards. It is the exclusive supplier of television programmes to its Zee TV satellite channel, offering six original hours each day, and it is planning to spin off a music channel independently. Zee, whose most popular programme is the much-watched *Banegi Apni Bat*, enjoys a profitable partnership with News Corporation, through Essel.

## PAINT
Asian Paints and other companies in the sector have had the benefit of a cut in excise duty of something in the region of 100 per cent. Another boost has been a turnaround in those industries that use paint, such as construction, automobiles and white goods.

## PAPER
The key paper companies of interest are Ballarpur Industries, ITC Bhadrachalam and Seshasayee Paper & Paper Board Ltd. Strong paper and newsprint prices during the last few years have made some of the new maharajahs involved in this sector quite a bit richer. There is, however, a real need for capital expenditure to bring the equipment up to date. Agro-based paper mills will have to invest heavily in items like chemical-recovery systems, but this will only be possible if they increase capacity proportionately to cover cost.

## PHARMACEUTICALS
The success of this sector, and those involved in it, is dictated entirely by the global drug economies. Not surprisingly it is a foreign company, Glaxo, that is the largest player in terms of market share, with about 5 per cent of the retail formulations market. This is because India has a strict price-control regime in which small-scale units have

111

traditionally been exempt from excise duty. At the moment, however, there are a number of mergers and acquisitions taking place which are consolidating the sector. One example is the Piramals' acquisition of Sumitra Pharma. The multinational corporations are regrouping in response and are setting up 100 per cent subsidiaries, both for the launch of new products and for research and development. Expenditure on R&D has been poor among the home-grown companies, partly because they have long enjoyed considerable protection through the process patent regime, whereby they could copy drugs at fractional prices. When India adopts international product patent standards in the year 2005, this will all change, and thus Indian companies will need to do some catching up before then. It takes an average $30 million internationally to discover a new drug, but costs are cheaper in India. Since 50 per cent of R&D funds goes on indirect costs, such as interest, Indian companies, with their lower base cost, should be able to make headway.

It is interesting to note that the government accounts for only around one-third of the national expenditure on healthcare. The breakdown in products bought shows that 23.2 per cent are antibiotics and antibacterials, 6 per cent vitamins, 5 per cent cough and cold remedies, 5 per cent anti-inflammatory drugs, 3.4 per cent anti-tuberculosis, 3 per cent analgesics and 3 per cent cardiovascular related. The key new maharajahs' companies are Ranbaxy, Core Healthcare and Dr Reddy's. The latter is very strong indeed in the process engineering of pharmaceutical products. Although it has high operating margins and large research and development expenditure, it is in a strong position to tap into the growth of the generic products market.

POWER

Power in India is always a problem, so those companies situated in states fortunate enough to have reliable generation have a significant advantage. Those able to achieve self-sufficiency, as some companies do, can maintain a commanding position in their industry. The Hindujas, in collaboration with the UK's National Power, have built a 1,000 MW coal-fired power plant in Vishakhapatnam in Andhra Pradesh. Srichand Hinduja points to the 'enormous difficulty' of having to deal with four different chief ministers of the state over a two-year period, maintaining nevertheless that progress has been satisfactory. The Birlas became involved in this sector, like many others, as part of a programme of vertical integration for a core company, aiming to reduce costs, achieve higher margins and ensure a reliable supply for production. Some 10.7 per cent of the total Tata Group turnover comes from its power-related activities, and they sell power to bulk consumers in Bombay, and the Essar Group too have companies involved in power generation.

Even in the most optimistic of scenarios, India is bound to face continued power shortages over the next five years. Subsidised tariffs, fuel supply constraints and state regulation will continue to cause problems for those new maharajahs venturing into the sector. There continue to be very few private electric utilities in India, and 96 per cent of capacity is government-owned. Incentives offered to the private sector have brought a flood of proposals, but delays in government approval often put people off. The central government utilities are purely generating companies, with the state electricity boards generating and distributing power within their respective states. Most power plants in India are coal-based, largely due to the abundant coal reserves, which are estimated to be sufficient for another 280 years, while the shortage of gas means that there are few gas-based plants. Despite the vast potential for hydro power, this resource remains neglected, because it takes longer to develop and the capital required is very much greater. Nuclear power does not at present appear to be an option, due to safety and money considerations, but this may well change any day.

While demand for power has grown at 9 per cent over the past ten years, capacity has not kept pace, and India now faces an estimated demand-supply gap of 9 per cent and a peaking shortage of over 20 per cent. The energy shortage varies from region to region, with the south suffering the highest deficit in absolute terms, and the east having the highest percentage of shortage, at about 14 per cent. There is no national grid for the transfer of excess electricity from one region to another. The poor quality and unreliability of public supplies has led to the development of private captive power generation, estimated to be 9,500 MW.

Power has to be any Indian government's first infrastructural priority for the rest of this decade, and is expected to attract the largest amount of private money. Most private investors, however, are waiting to feel the political pulse, and with only an estimated 20,000 MW to be added in the next five years, the power situation is destined to get worse.

## PROPERTY

Ghanshyam Sheth, of the Sheth shipping dynasty, runs the family's foray into property and development. Like a number of new maharajahs, the family got into property at the end of the 1980s in a bid to diversify and minimise their exposure to the downturn in their core business. Their innate ability as traders should, they believe, translate well from one sector into another, and they are working hard to establish a position at the top end of the market. Many others dabble on different scales in both the commercial and residential sectors.

## RETAIL

All around Asia, the 'mom and pop' store is a prominent feature of everyday life, and nowhere is this more true than in India. They provide access in the most remote of villages to a whole host of products, although these have to have a relatively long shelf life, because turnover is much slower than we are used to in the West. Sales from these small stores form a critical part of the distribution chain, and it will probably be some considerable time before more modern methods of retailing are seen in the country at large. In the major cities, however, department stores and specialist niche-market retailers are apparently doing well.

## STEEL

In terms of demand for crude steel, Japan, Korea and the United States are the world's largest consumers. India comes only eleventh, with the country's per capital steel consumption of 22 kg only 15 per cent of the world average and 22 per cent of the average per capita consumption of other Asian countries. In addition, the intensity of steel consumption – which is one of the strongest indicators of the growth potential for demand – is also extremely low. Over the last fifty years the Indian steel industry has had a history of regulation, with the government forbidding the creation of new integrated steel plants in the private sector and running an elaborate price-fixing scheme under which existing companies had to sell their products. Since liberalisation in 1991, licensing regulations have been eased, and most of the taxes imposed either reduced or removed.

Those new maharajahs such as the Kalyanis, the Ruias, the Birlas and the Tata Group with interests in the steel sector are in for a rosy time, since the low per capita consumption and steel intensity serve only to underscore the strong growth potential for the product in the country. With continuing investment in infrastructural projects and the growing demand for automobiles and consumer goods, demand can only grow vigorously. Labour costs for producers are, however, like everything else, in India, on the rise, and there is a great deal of negotiation still to be done with labour unions. Another significant factor for producers is the decontrol of the price of coking coal, which makes up nearly half of the expenditure on raw materials required in the process.

The larger steel plants with integrated production are clearly in a much stronger position than smaller ones, because of the ever-increasing cost of power. Heavy fuel price increases across the board have been compounded by a new tax. The small plants which will continue to do well are those producing value-added steel products like stainless steel and alloy steel, since they are insulated somewhat from the rising steel scrap prices and spiralling power costs. Integrated steel producers too will have a strong competitive advantage over imports from outside India. Many steel producers, such as the Ruias of Essar Steel, are planning significant capacity expansion that may well lead to oversupply, at a time when international steel demand could continue to flatten and prices stay down. The future profitability of Essar is said to depend on a key hot strip mill project that has been subject so far to a great deal of delay. However, the fluctuations of the rupee in the currency market often insulate domestic steel manufacturers against declining prices.

TELECOMMUNICATIONS
Another high priority for any government in India has to be telecommunications, and outlay in this sector has recently been trebled, with plans afoot to intall ten million lines. Telecommunications services have for a very long time been governed by state monopoly, but recent partial privatisation has allowed the private sector into basic telecommunications services. The government's Department of Telecommunications and the quasi-government Mahanagar Telephone Nigam Ltd. account for over 90 per cent of telephone cable sales. Until 1984, cable was reserved for the public sector, and even today the state-owned Hindustan Cables Ltd. remains the dominant presence in 'jelly filled telecom cables'. Sterlite and Finolex are the two largest private-sector JFTC manufacturers, with a total capacity of 65 million cable kilometers. This is much more than existing demand, since private telecom operators cannot use JFTC in their

networks and are required to utilise fibre-optic cables or wireless technology, except in the last 500 metres of the local loop.

The biggest players in telecommunications amongst new maharajahs are the Ambanis, who have a tie-up with Nyex Corporation of the United States. One of many moving into the sector, Aditya Birla's son, Kumar Managalam, plans to enter basic telecom services in partnership with American company AT&T. It is no surprise that the Hindujas are also in the telecommunications sector, since it is their policy to focus on key infrastructural businesses. In the late 1980s they completed a proposal in partnership with the UK's Cable & Wireless which was, they believe, killed off because of India's protected systems. As a result, they argue, the country lost an opportunity to modernise its telecommunications structure in an efficient way. More recently, the family has been trying to collaborate with Singapore Telecom in a tender for the privatisation of basic services. However, the government perceived the attempt as a wholly foreign investment and so rejected the overture. Telecommunications are also on the agenda for the Mittals, who are planning to expand in the sector. Tata Telecom Ltd. too has entered into an alliance with a number of international companies, and Thapar, one of India's oldest and largest conglomerates, has also diversified into the sector. The Ruias are another family trying hard to be significant players in the telecommunications industry, and to this end their Essar Group has joined up with Bell Atlantic of the USA to bid for basic and value-added services.

TEXTILES
The three key companies in cotton textiles are the Ambanis' Reliance, Bombay Dyeing, and the Birlas' Grasim. Reliance is said to be facing problems with pricing because of a possible threat to its profits from imported polymers, which have traditionally constituted nearly one-third of its turnover. Grasim, on the other hand, which is facing strong demand for its rayon as cotton prices rise, has undergone a capacity expansion. The key companies in polyester are Arvind Mills and Century Textiles, while in polyester yarn and fibre the main players are Sanghi Polyester, DCL Polyester and, of course, Reliance Industries.

Chapter 7

# Caste: The League in the Indian Game

There are many issues for the foreign business traveller to grasp about India's complex society – the differences between Hindu, Muslim and Sikh, between Bengali, Punjabi and Tamil – but the hardest division for Westerners to come to terms with is that of caste. This artificial division of society was probably first made known as early as 1516 by the Portuguese writer Barbosa, who described the distinct *castas* among the Indian people. This Portuguese word meaning 'breed', 'race' or 'kind' has been retained in English in the belief that it was the native term.

No single business giant in this book could be said to have got where he is, or not got where he wants to be, because of his position in society. Out of 920 million people, these are the inevitable commercial stars who would doubtless succeed under any social, political or economic regime. However, since Brahmins often seek work abroad, many of the new maharajahs in the diaspora are from that particular caste. The Brahmins are said to have an unwritten rule that states that they should get out of India and stay out, and inevitably this has created an immense brain-drain. While the population of Tamil Nadu, for example, has more than doubled over the last fifty years, the number of Brahmins in the state has decreased by a third. They have fled to a better life and greater freedom elsewhere.

While it is the slums and the beggars that most horrify visitors to the subcontinent, it is caste that causes society itself its greatest problems. The basic cause of poverty in developing countries is usually considered to be the economic backwardness or stagnation of the rural areas where the vast majority of the population live. In India the income of agricultural workers is substantially below the national average, and is often almost at subsistence level. In the cities,

117

although the slums contain widespread poverty, there is at least start-ing to exist a real and quite new freedom. The inside of many of these slum dwellings is scrupulously clean and tidy. Each morning some of the children go off to school in neat uniforms. The few people who have saved enough money to return to their villages rarely do so. For them, city life is better, and not just because they have earned enough to buy a radio or a bicycle. In the city, despite a recent politicisation of caste, the grip of the system is beginning to ease. In the years of economic liberalisation since 1991, artificial constructs for society have become increasingly irrelevant. As new types of occupation have arisen, the old divisions of caste have become less clear-cut, and with the growth of the private sector, new possibilities have opened up for people. Few are better positioned to capitalise on the move towards a meritocracy than the new maharajahs, and it is to them that falls the real task of revolutionising India. By creating a modern com-mercial society, discrimination and persistent poverty may for the first time in the country's history be tackled effectively.

There are many reasons why people are fleeing the rural areas where 70 per cent of India's vast population still live. By and large people remain what their ancestors were, since that is what the system dictates, and that usually means fixed in illiteracy and poverty. The economically unviable size of land holdings, which are still decreasing as a result of the system of dividing property among many, makes it well-nigh impossible to achieve anything other than the barest subsistence living, while the lack of irrigation means that farmers are dependent on rainfall and the vagaries of nature. The vast majority lack sufficient financial resources to invest in seeds, manure or equipment, or to pay seasonal labour costs. There is no satisfactory administrative system such as cooperatives to organise the purchase and resale of agricultural produce, and the lack of transport facilities and a good road network hinders the rapid distribution of fresh veg-etables and fruit. Many small farmers and unskilled agricultural labourers are ill-equipped for alternative employment in related sec-tors which could provide a source of income during the slack season, and so they turn to the cities. Once there, although some rural people do tend to be conservative and traditional in their outlook, and resist attempts to change their social behaviour and attitudes, many others are beginning to show distinct signs of wanting to break free of their familiar constraints.

It is essential that anyone seeking to do business in India has at least a basic understanding of the caste system. The premise is that every man, whether a distinguished multinational entrepreneur or a street-sweeper on the roads of Calcutta, is accorded his place in the universe at birth. In rural areas particularly, caste shapes almost every aspect of life: the food that may be eaten and who cooks it, the colour and length of a sari, how a dhoti is tied, how a bath is taken, and whether or not someone may carry an umbrella. Rules are even applied to the way a man's moustache may be trained. By the beginning of the next century, however, something in the region of 350 million Indians will live in cities, where the niceties of the caste system simply cannot work. A Brahmin on a packed bus, for instance, cannot jump off and bathe six times because he fears the shadow of an Untouchable has fallen on him. He cannot always be sure who has cooked his food, where his water has come from, or whether the job he needs to pay the rent will satisfy caste rules.

The structure of Hinduism, to which the caste system is fundamental, has nothing in common with the prescribed ranks of other religions, for each man decides for himself which aspects of the deities are most crucial to him. The individual has a substantial degree of autonomy in deciding which doctrines to follow and whose personal example to imitate. The hierarchy of the caste system is thought to have been first established 4,000 years ago when, at the time of the Aryan invasion, the light-skinned northerners wanted to distinguish themselves from the dark-skinned Dravidians. It is thought that the idea was to keep the indigenous peoples in their place.

Generally speaking Hindus are classified by *varna*, derived from the Sanskrit word for colour. The main division is between the Forward Castes and the Backward Castes. The Forwards are said to be those castes at the upper end of the Vedic or ritual scale. They are usually better educated and as such hold higher positions. Included in this group are the Brahmins, the scholar priests, who, while the best schooled, are not necessarily the wealthiest. The Rajputs, a particularly successful branch of the Kshatriya class, traditionally warriors and kings, are also Forward, as are the Vaisyas or businessmen, while the Backward Castes comprise the Sudras, or labourers, and the Untouchables, now also known as the Scheduled Castes. Of India's 100 million Untouchables, 85 per cent live in rural areas. It is these unfortunates who have the worst jobs in society, those that are considered too polluting, both spiritually and literally, for other Hindus.

Among the various subdivisions of the Untouchables are the

119

Doums, who take care of all of India's cremations, while the lowliest of the low are the Bhangis, or sewage scavengers, so ostracised that not even the tanners and animal cremators – Untouchables themselves – will go near them. Segregated even within the slums, India's 700,000 scavengers earn pennies a day moving the flow of human waste for a country in which 650 million people still lack access to basic sanitation.

There are distinctions in the castes from area to area; in the south of the country, for example, Brahmins are rigidly vegetarian, whereas in Bengal they eat fish and in Kashmir they eat meat. 'High-caste' does not necessarily mean people of top rank: destitute Brahmins are common. Neither are the castes themselves rigid. The Kshatriya caste has ceased to be a 'warrior' grouping but has become the label for those of lower ranking who have made good, either by force or by sheer native wit.

As far as Vedic law is concerned, one's lot in life may improve, or worsen, depending on deeds done in a lifetime. The fact that a person is born into one caste or another is not seen as an accident of fate but as a carefully orchestrated plan by the deities as a reward or punishment for actions in a past life. If morals are not adhered to there is punishment: marrying or having children by someone from a different caste may result in rebirth as an Untouchable. Across India, caste is a major factor in determining marriage partners. Under the widely used system of family-arranged marriages, young people are only betrothed to partners of the same caste.

According to the most recently available statistics, from the 1980 Mandal Report, the top castes in India make up only 17.6 per cent of the population, while the Backward Castes constitute 43.7 per cent. Prior to this, the last time that caste was included in an Indian census was in 1931. Later governments, hoping perhaps that it would go away, just ignored it, but its grip on society is far too strong for that.

The castes are further subdivided into thousands of *jati*, groups that are geographically defined and classified according to occupation, with members bound together by the fact that their fathers followed the same profession. Those in the top subdivisions have no involvement in physical work of any kind, while the lowest do menial tasks such as laundry or cutting people's hair and beards. Today *jati* seems to predominate over *varna*, since this fellowship gives individuals a sense of belonging and support, and is the closest thing in India to a genuine welfare system.

The commission after the Mandal Report proposed that there should be massive discrimination in favour of the Backward Castes. Reform has often been attempted, beginning most notably at the start of the nineteenth century with Rajah Ram Mohan Roy, the ruler of Bengal, who founded the Brahmo Samaj movement, hoping to blend a reformed Hinduism with Western ethics. He believed that only when Hinduism had cleansed itself of caste prejudice and the oppression of women would India be strong enough to throw off the intruding British.

Mahatma Gandhi was in many ways a spiritual descendant of Roy. He wanted to make life better for his countrymen as much as he wanted the British out of India, and he campaigned tirelessly to improve the lot of the Untouchables – or, as he called them, the Harijans, the children of God. The practice of untouchability – that is, of avoiding all contact with people of the lowest castes – was nominally outlawed after India became independent, and a system of quotas was laid down in the constitution which, however, was never meant to turn into the permanent, legally prescribed system that it has become.

The result in everyday terms of the caste system is a multi-layered social hierarchy that has developed over thousands of years and is still strongly adhered to. Caste offers a secular means of organising people into different roles, and it also allows the powers-that-be to create order where there could so easily otherwise be chaos. Sadly, it provides too the perfect mechanism for mass exploitation.

Most Indians agree that unless there is some radical reform of the caste system, large proportions of society will be left indefinitely as powerless pariahs. The Backward Castes, who form a substantial proportion of India's population, have the vote and are using it, with the result that caste, instead of withering away as a political factor, as the founding fathers of independent India had hoped, has sprung to life again. Caste can decide who wins elections in India today.

Since Independence, the major political parties have periodically promised to do something about caste, but nothing actually happened until 1990, when V. P. 'Rajah' Singh of the Janata Dal Party implemented reforms. His changes were made with an important political aim in mind: by appealing to the Backward Castes he hoped to cut into the vote of the Bharatiya Janata Party (BJP), then the rising star of Indian politics. The BJP like to present themselves as the champions of all Hindus, but the party still has a strong upper-caste flavour.

The protection that the Indian constitution offers to Untouchables is part of Gandhi's legacy. Today they have reserved seats in the lower houses of both the central and the state legislatures, a quota of government jobs, and reserved places at schools and colleges. The upper orders have never quite accepted this, and there has developed an aggressive 'affirmative action programme' to enforce the quotas. Critics argue, however, that protection for the Untouchables has resulted not in labour and social freedom but in an increased dependency on welfare for some who are not genuinely in need. Furthermore, it has actually strengthened the caste system and its inherent apartheid, and could even be said to have caused many people, especially in the civil service, to work less hard.

India's central bureaucracy plays a key role in holding the country together. Recruitment on any basis except merit would be folly, yet Untouchables are guaranteed 22.5 per cent of government jobs. Air India, for example, the country's national airline, has a written and legally enforceable rule that a member of a 'Backward Caste must be promoted after five years without regard for merit or seniority'. However, nearly all Indians have the idea instilled into them from birth that life is inherently unfair, and so rules, rewards and punishments are widely accepted with little argument.

Since the country became independent, a great many positive changes have taken place. The population is now self-sufficient in terms of food, an achievement which is due in large part to the implementation of the Green Revolution policy in the winter of 1967–8. In that year the first big crop of Mexican-bred dwarf wheat was planted in the Punjab, leading to bumper crops each year since, and the quintupling of the country's annual wheat output. Progress has not just come in agriculture either: industrially speaking India stands in ninth position in the world in terms of output. It could also be said that a great many Indians are modern-day thinkers, taking enlightened positions with regard to revolutionising attitudes. However, only a very small number seem to be aware of the reform that must now be necessary to the caste system.

India's religious minorities are also affected by the caste system. Sikhs, Muslims and Christians feature as honorary castes. The Sikh scripture, the *Guru Granth Sahib*, preaches equality, and at their temples Jats and Harijans pray together, all wearing beards and turbans. In Goa's Christian churches, though, there are always two doors: one for Brahmins and another for the rest. With the sharpening of caste-consciousness, sectarian strife is rampant, and the Muslims of Karnataka were just one of the many groups of vicitms of recent Hindu violence. In general, Muslims, who used to vote Congress but were outraged by the prime minister's behaviour during the crisis over the Ayodhya mosque in 1992, have turned instead to the Janata Dal Party and others like it, and with pro-Muslim parties in power, bridges are being built between Muslims and Hindus in the areas where the worst disputes between them took place not long ago.

It is unquestionably true that India's government could more effectively provide opportunities to members of lower castes by improving the education system. All that the current policy of affirmative action is doing is sharpening class-consciousness and causing political division between castes. As we have seen, V. P. Singh tried to rally the Backward Castes to his Janata Dal Party. Redress was attempted subsequently by Narasimha Rao, who tried to reserve 10 per cent of jobs for poor members of the upper castes, only for the Supreme Court to rule this unconstitutional. The widespread unpopularity of his efforts played a large part in turning a great many people against the Congress Party and towards the right-wing Bharatiya Janata Party, who were keen to win the votes of the lower castes and religious minorities.

Some 113 people died in the city of Nagpur in Maharashtra state when 40,000 members of the Gowari tribe (traditionally cow-herders for the Gond caste), protested against their exlusion from quota rights. They demanded improved conditions, only to be set upon by the police in an over-reactive panic. The difference in punctuation between a statement that read 'GondGowari' (sic) and 'Gond, Gowari' was at the centre of the bloodshed. A simple comma was, the Gowaris well knew, reason for them to be excluded from affirmative action privileges. The Gonds had the power to fight the bureaucratic bungle and did so. The Gowaris did not. This was just one of very many similarly bloody incidents which continue to this day, including one in Uttar Pradesh involving the Yadavs and the rape of two dozen women and the injury of 150 others protesting their caste misfortunes. Incidentally, it is the Yadavs, the traditional cow-herders, who in many areas of the country are considered to be the new boys on the block. They are said to possess an extreme willingness to use violence, and they are sometimes portrayed as the meanest and toughest of the caste armies that control most aspects of life in a number of states.

There has also been a wave of self-immolations by members of the 'Forward Castes' who had been displaced. Just one of many of these incidents was when Rajiv Goswami, a Brahmin from a respectable middle-class Punjabi family, went on prolonged hunger strike, and then set himself on fire with kerosene. Yet his life had not been particularly miserable. His father worked as a clerk in the post office and he had earned a place at college. However, mercifully he lived to tell the tale. Another victim Sursala Mohan, a twenty year old in Hyderabad, did not. Such were the feelings of indignation that violent protest was often regarded as the only course of action to take. Goswami and Mohan felt that they had no future since the jobs that had previously been assured to them by caste decree, in central government, had disappeared before their very eyes to a member of the Backward Castes.

In Bihar, a rich farming state north-west of Delhi, the caste on the make is the Haryana. The Jats there, having benefited mightily from the green revolution, displaced the Rajputs as the dominant caste years ago. Their leader is Devi Lal, a semi-literate giant of a man. While he was the state's chief minister, Devi Lal put no fewer than 133 of his relatives into senior government jobs. On joining the national government he made his son chief minister of Haryana without bothering to consult the voters.

There is also a new separatist movement in India – apart from the issue of Kashmir – that once just bubbled below the surface but is now on fire. Take the Punjab as an example. There is a clear majority of Punjabis, including many, perhaps most, Sikh Jats, who do not want a separate Sikh state. The caste system though has thrown evil upon evil with agricultural workers out of jobs and prevented from doing anything other than emigrating, for example, to the Gulf, for work. Many complain that Delhi's Brahmin rulers have neglected the Punjab because of the predominance there of people from other castes. Violence is, for the unemployed, poorly educated young Jat a means of immediate and powerful expression.

In the final analysis, the issue of caste has become a political football, useful for those cynical politicians looking for any way of securing votes and power. The majority of Indians support political candidates from their own castes because such candidates are more likely to push through changes that directly and positively affect their lives. Political parties formed by such single-issue candidates are more likely to succeed, and until educational or other real reform is enacted, there is little hope of improvement.

Caste divisions are, however, now weakening in the cities in the face of growing Western influence. Signs of modern wealth – such as Kentucky Fried Chicken outlets and mobile phones – are starting to appear, and when young urban people marry they no longer insist on a partner from their own caste, being more likely to desire a mate who is elegantly dressed or who drives a good car. Money is the newest social distinction, though even in the cities intercaste marriage with an Untouchable will remain unheard of as long as superstition and tradition dominate. Nothing will change until people stop believing in reincarnation and start believing in themselves.

Caste has gradually changed from a system apparently designed to assert genetic superiority to a method of distributing political spoils. The fact that India is a genuine democracy, where every person, at least in principle, commands a vote equal to everybody else's, means that all the old patterns of her society are being eroded, while at the same time urbanisation is also eating away at the caste system. At last a modern commercial society is looming, and the new maharajahs are leading the way.

# Appendix 1:

# A Business Briefing

## (I) GUIDE TO INDIA

Those travelling to the subcontinent will notice that economic progress in India, Pakistan and Bangladesh has generally been slower than in many other developing countries. This is in large part due to the vogue for socialism at the time of Independence. The government of the time devised heavy-duty industrial plans so that the state could control the economy. In India, from Independence until 1977, overall growth was about 3.5 per cent a year. In the years of Indira Gandhi's rule, however, and those of her son, Rajiv, there was a change of direction. In the Seventh Five-Year Plan (1986–90) the emphasis was laid on industrial liberalisation and modernisation, on the need to develop an export culture instead of relying on import substitution. There were also plans to generate employment, develop agriculture in low-production areas, improve the manufacture of basic goods and reduce poverty. Rajiv Gandhi also welcomed new overseas investment, largely because India's budget deficit and foreign debts tend to grow at alarming rates. Prime Minister Rao's programme of liberalisation speeded up improvements even further. Progress, albeit slow, has been made in agriculture, and due to the spread of irrigation India has become almost self-sufficient in food production. Rao's reforms spurred overseas investment in India, and since July 1991 – when the free-market reform policy was first implemented – there have been well over 20,000 foreign investment proposals filed with the government, worth in excess of $140 billion.

Against this background, it should be said that in the short term, business prospects for outsiders will for some time remain almost totally dependent on choice of product line. Those interested in involvement in a power plant, for example, in telecommunications

126

or other infrastructural projects, or in any export-orientated enterprise will find business unexpectedly easy. The specific areas which
offer a great chance of success are:

Aircraft and parts
Biotechnology
Chemical-production machinery
Computer software and services
Electric power systems
Food-processing and packaging equipment
Hotel and restaurant equipment
Laboratory and scientific equipment
Machine tools
Medical instruments and equipment
Metalworking equipment
Mining-industry equipment
Oil-field and gas-field machinery and services
Pollution-control equipment
Railroad equipment
Renewable-energy equipment
Scientific and industrial fibre-optics
Telecommunications equipment
Textile machinery and equipment

Many of these sectors are well on their way to high standards of
development but need cutting-edge technology and skills transfer.
The subcontinent generally is trying to upgrade infrastructure, industrial base and standards of living, but modern techniques and expertise are not widely available from local companies. Clearly, it is
essential to do your homework before taking the plunge into commercial involvement in India.

## The Correct Business Approach

The most daunting aspect of business on the subcontinent, and particularly in India, is the bureaucracy. Few Westerners will have
encountered anything quite like it before. While red tape is beginning
to release its tight grip on the economy, the bureaucrats still wield
great power, compounding existing inefficiencies. The key to success
lies in planning and an approach to decision-making that bears in
mind the bureaucratic pitfalls. The kind of decisions affected are loca-

tion, choice of partner in any joint venture and hiring of personnel.

The three key considerations for location are incentives, infrastructure and local politics. Individual states usually compete for foreign investment by offering subsidies, sales tax exemptions, power concessions and tax holidays.

In some cases – foreign affairs, customs duties and taxation of income, for instance – central government has exclusive territory to make and enforce laws, but aspects such as labour welfare and price controls are managed at both local and national level. The granting of business licences can therefore be tricky, since permission may be granted by either of the two levels, and in some cases by both. Although local expertise and guidance is widely available, outsiders are liable to be frustrated by the lack of any urgency or speed in local government and by the absence of synchronisation in the bureaucratic process.

In approaching and attempting to work with state governments, it is as well to note that some are a great deal more friendly and efficient than others. Even with the best of them, though, there are still issues that a foreign business entity needs to consider before setting up. The prime consideration, bar none, is the question of power. An efficient business cannot function without some kind of assurance of power supply, something that cannot be taken for granted in India. Just to get a connection may take anything up to eighteen months and require several dozen forms to be filled out. The same is true of telecommunications, water and the land itself. Then there are ecological and environmental requirements and permissions, and the tricky issue of employing locals in accordance with the labour laws. With proof of compliance with laws an essential aspect of running a business, it is no surprise that the professionals available to undertake such work are in great demand with the foreign community.

The key way to circumvent bureaucracy is through a liaison with a local company, perhaps one of the new maharajahs. Besides the common business criteria used to evaluate a good partner – compatability, commitment, combined strength – the ability of the local business to work the bureaucratic process should be taken into consideration. The opportunity to form joint ventures with Indian industrial groups is not restricted to large multinational corporations alone. Smaller companies can benefit by partnering a firm within these groups. It is important to keep in mind that a company that has served as an agent or representative may not necessarily be the best choice for a partner in a joint venture. Though these companies may have served as capable middlemen in export-import transactions, they might not have the necessary experience or resources to be a full partner. It is also essential to consider whether real compatability in business philosophy is possible.

It can be a good idea to hire expatriate employees of Indian origin to head operations in India. These managers have the dual advantage of knowing both the company and the culture of the country. Cultural literacy programmes should be offered to those new to India, to help them understand what they will be dealing with. Of prime concern are the cultural, social and business customs of the country, such as the Indian work clock: the business day tends to begin at around 9.30 a.m. rather than 7.30 or 8.00, when most expatriates are accustomed to beginning work. Dress is another source of concern, and it is a relief to know that with the heat there is no rigid dress code in Indian business circles.

## The Electoral System

The Indian political system is not a complex one to Western minds. The head of state is nominally the president, but true power lies with the prime minister, who controls the Lok Sabha – the House of the People – which contains 546 members elected by universal suffrage for a five-year term. At each election, the president is theoretically and by legal mandate given the reins of power for six years. The Rajya Sabha – or Upper House – is made up of 250 members, twelve of them nominated by the president and the rest elected by state legislatures for six-year terms. Every one of India's states has its own governor, and an elected state assembly with a chief minister and a council of ministers.

## Cities and Towns

The main cities are: Delhi (population 6 million); Calcutta, the capital of West Bengal (13 million if Greater Calcutta is included); Bombay, the capital of Maharashtra (8.5 million if Greater Bombay is included); Madras, the capital of Tamil Nadu (4.5 million); Hyderabad, the capital of Andhra Pradesh (3 million if Secunderabad is included); Bangalore, India's 'Silicon Valley', in Karnataka (3 million); Ahmedabad, in Gujarat (2.5 million); Kanpur, in Uttar Pradesh (1.6 million); Pune in Maharashtra (1.7 million). There are said to be some 596,000 villages in India. International trade fairs and shows tend to be held in Bombay and New Delhi, though some are now held in Bangalore.

## Publications

One of the largest-circulation newspapers is the *Indian Express*, published in ten different editions. The *Hindustan Times* is the leading Delhi newspaper, and *The Times of India* the main Bombay daily. There are literally hundreds of other local daily newspapers, in a variety of languages, with well over 200 in Hindi alone. For the best business news, the three daily financial newspapers published in English are the *Economic Times* (Delhi, Bombay and Calcutta), the *Financial Express* (Delhi, Madras and Bombay) and the *Business Standard of Calcutta*. Business periodicals include *Capital* (Calcutta), *Commerce, Business India, Business World* and *Update* (Bombay). India has one of the finest collections of home-grown trade publications anywhere, covering any number of industrial and service sectors in great detail.

## Broadcasting

There are still only 17.5 million television sets in India, and approximately 65 million radios. The government-run radio station broadcasts around the clock, and All-India Television now airs for most of the day.

## Climate

Mainly tropical, but varies greatly from the extreme heat of the tropics in the south and the desert in the north-west, to the extreme cold of the northern Himalayas. November to March is bright and dry in the south but cold in the north. Bombay is hot and humid; Delhi is dry. April to June is hot and dry throughout much of the country, though more temperate and cool in the far north. There are heavy monsoons in the south-west in June and in the south-east in October and November.

## Entry Requirements

A passport is required by all except certain seamen. Nationals of all countries except Bhutan and Nepal also need visas, and additional visas may be required for re-entry by visitors to some neighbouring countries, such as Nepal, Sri Lanka, Afghanistan, Burma and Bangladesh.

## Health Requirements

Vaccination certificates for yellow fever are required if travelling from an infected area. It is advisable to be vaccinated against cholera, hepatitis and tetanus, and to take anti-malarial precautions. Avoid unboiled drinking water. Salt loss should be replaced by taking extra salt with meals.

## Transport

There are a number of international airports: Babatpur (VNS), 22.5 km from Varanasi; Sahar International (BOM), 25 km north of Bombay, with duty-free shop, bar, restaurant, currency exchange, post office; Dum Dum (CCU), 13 km north-east of Calcutta, with duty-free shop, bar, restaurant, buffet, bank, hotel reservations, post office, shops; Meenambakkam (MAA), 14 km south-east of Madras, with duty-free shop, restaurant, buffet, bank, hotel reservations, post office, shops; Indira Gandhi International Airport (DEL), 20 km south of Delhi, with duty-free shop, restaurant, buffet, bank, post office; Patna (PAT), 6 km from Patna. Indian Airlines, the country's domestic carrier, operate over a hundred flights daily, with services linking all main cities.

The main sea ports are Bombay, Calcutta, Cochin, Kandla, Madras, Mangalore, Marmagao and Vishakhapatnam.

There are 1,772,200 kilometres of road, with 833,000 km of surfaced roads and 32,138 km of national highways connecting the main cities. Self-drive hire cars are available in Bombay, but are not a wise choice. Chauffeur-driven cars and vans are available for hire in major cities. Local taxis of varying standards are also usually available. Meters, however, are unlikely to be working, and fares should always be negotiated in advance. Tipping is officially discouraged, but is in practice discretionary.

Rail is the main form of domestic transport. The Indian railway network covers over 63,000 km, and connections are available between all major towns and cities, with reconditioned coaches and sleeper accommodation on some routes.

## Hotels

International-standard accommodation is widely available. Hotel bills must be paid in foreign currency, or in rupees proved to have been purchased in India with foreign exchange, which can be a lengthy procedure. Hotels in the main cities are usually heavily

131

booked, and it is advisable to make reservations well in advance. It may be necessary to take your own bedding when visiting upcountry hotels and rest houses.

## Credit Cards
Major credit cards, such as American Express, Diners Club and Visa are accepted by international hotels, travel agencies and airline offices, as well as some larger stores. The Central Card issued by the Bank of India, is also widely accepted.

## Public Holidays
1 January (New Year)
26 January (Republic Day)
1 May (May Day)
15 August (Independence Day)
2 October (Gandhi's birthday)
25 and 26 December (Christmas)

## Working Hours
*Business (Mon–Fri)*
Delhi and Madras: 10 a.m. to 5 p.m.; Calcutta: 9.30 a.m. to 5 p.m.; Bombay: 10 a.m. to 5.30 p.m.
*Government (Mon–Fri)*
Delhi, Calcutta and Madras: 9 a.m. to 5.30 p.m.; Bombay: 9.30 a.m. to 4.30 p.m.
*Banking (Mon–Fri)*
Delhi, Calcutta and Madras: 10 a.m. to 2 p.m. (Sat 10 a.m. to 12 noon); Bombay: 11 a.m. to 3 p.m. (Sat 11 a.m. to 1 p.m.)
*Shops (Mon–Sat)*
Delhi: 9.30 a.m. to 7.30 p.m.; Calcutta and Bombay: 10 a.m. to 6.30 p.m.; Madras: 9 a.m. to 7.30 p.m.

## Social Customs
Cows are sacred to Hindus, and many Hindus are vegetarians. Sikhs and Parsees do not smoke tobacco. Muslims do not eat pig's flesh in any form, and orthodox Muslims do not drink alcoholic beverages.

## Telephone
Dialling code for India: IDD access code (00 from the UK) followed by 91, followed by area code:

Bangalore **80**
Bombay **22**
Calcutta **33**
New Delhi **11**
Madras **44**
(NB: Time zone is GMT + 5.5 hours)

## Electricity Supply
The supply is nearly always dubious except in big cities and international hotels (which have their own power supply). The current runs at 220 volts AC, 50 cycles (sometimes DC), for domestic use; 440 volts AC, 50 cycles 3-phase for industrial use.

## Weights and Measures
Metric system.

## Banking
Bombay is India's financial centre for all banking and other fiscal purposes. The central bank is the Reserve Bank of India. There are numerous public-sector banks, and also a number of private institutions. The following may be of interest:

The Bank of Cochin
The Bank of Rajasthan
Bareilly Corporation Bank
The Benares State Bank
Bharat Overseas Bank
Bank of Tamilnad
Bank of Thanjavur
The Catholic Syrian Bank
The Dhanalakshmi Bank
The Export-Import Bank of India
The Federal Jammu and Kashmir Bank
General Insurance Corp of India
Industrial Credit and Investment Corp of India
Industrial Development Bank
Industrial Finance Corp of India
Karnataka Bank
The Karur Vysya Bank
Kashi Nath Seth Bank

The Kumbakonam City Union Bank
The Lakshmi Bilas Bank
The Lakshmi Commercial Bank
Life Insurance Corp of India
Lord Krishna Bank
The Miraj State Bank
Nanital Bank
The Nedungadi Bank
The Parur Central Bank
The Purbancha Bank
The Ratnakar Bank
The Sangi Bank
The South Indian Bank
The Tamilnad Mercantile
The Traders Bank
United Industrial Bank
The United Western Bank
Unit Trust of India
The Vysya Bank

## International Organisations
India is a member of the following:

Asian Development Bank (ADB)
Colombo Plan
The Commonwealth
The EC Trade and Cooperation Agreement
Economic & Social Commission for Asia & the Pacific (ESCAP)
Food & Agriculture Organisation (FAO)
General Agreement on Tariffs & Trade (GATT)
Group of 7 (the finance ministers and central bankers of the US, Canada, Japan, Germany, France, Italy and the UK)
Inter-Governmental Organisation
Inter-Parliamentary Union (IPU)
International Air Transport Association (IATA)
International Atomic Energy Agency
International Bank for Reconstruction & Development (IBRD)
International Civil Aviation Organisation (ICAO)
International Development Association (IDA)
International Finance Corporation (IFC)

International Fund for Agricultural Development (IFAD)
International Hydog
International Labour Organisation
International Maritime Organisation (IMO)
International Monetary Fund (IMF)
International Lead & Zinc Study Group
International Red Cross (IRC)
International Telecommunications Union (ITU)
International Trade Commission (ITC)
Interpol
South Asian Association for Regional Cooperation
United Nations (UN)
United Nations Educational, Scientific and Cultural Organisation
(UNESCO)
United Nations Industrial Development Organisation (UNIDO)
Universal Postal Union (UPU)
World Bank
World Energy Conference (WEC)
World Federation of Trade Unions
World Health Organisation (WHO)
World Intellectual Property Organisation (WIPO)
World Meterological Organisation (WMO)
World Trade Organisation (WTO)

## (II) GUIDE TO PAKISTAN

Pakistan is the world's ninth most populous country, its population
having increased from 36 million in 1951 to nearly 110 million today.
The population density ranges from 230 per square kilometre in the
Punjab, to 12.5 per square kilometre in Baluchistan, and some 70 per
cent of people live in rural areas. About 44.5 per cent of the present
population is below fifteen years of age. Over 95 per cent of Pakistanis
are followers of the Islamic faith. There is no caste system as such on
the Indian model, but society has its own prescribed hierarchy.

Parliamentary democracy, with a civilian prime minister, was rein-
troduced in Pakistan in December 1985, although former military
dictator President Zia ul-Haq remained in power until his death in a
plane accident in August 1988. General elections followed in
November 1988. The federal parliament consists of a 237-seat
National Assembly and an 87-seat Senate. The president is elected for
a five-year term. The four provinces – Punjab, Sind, Baluchistan and

135

North-West Frontier – each have their own assemblies.

The Islamic Democratic Alliance (IDA), which was formed in 1988 from several right-wing parties to oppose the Pakistan People's Party (PPP), controls the Punjab, the biggest and most important province. The PPP advocates Islamic socialism, democracy and non-alignment. The Mohajir Qaumi Movement (MQM), which represents Muslim immigrants, has also risen to prominence since 1987. In addition there are a great many regional parties. The present prime minister is Benazir Bhutto. It was under her predecessor, Nawaz Sharif, that the country attempted to move towards economic liberalisation and the privatisation of a large number of public industries.

## Business Statistics

Pakistan's economy, like those of Bangladesh and India, is heavily dependent on agriculture. Setbacks to possible growth include warfare, political upheaval, poor weather, failing crops, rapid population growth and the burden of the country's three million refugees from Afghan. Although still predominantly agrarian in character, the economy has undergone significant changes in terms of growth, patterns of production and consumption, employment structure, the direction of foreign trade and the relative roles of the public and private sectors.

The contribution of agriculture to the GDP has declined from 53 per cent in 1949–50 to just under 30 per cent, with a corresponding rise in industry's contribution, from 9.6 per cent to almost 20 per cent. Pakistan has managed a self-sustained, broad-based growth rate of about 6 per cent per annum. Investment (16 per cent of GNP) and savings (12 per cent of GNP) are low in absolute terms as well as in comparison with the levels attained by other countries. Remittances from abroad, which have been a major source of foreign exchange, continue to be favourable after a brief slump. Export processing zones have been established and the procedure for foreign investment has been simplified. Inflation averages between 6 and 10 per cent per annum.

Unemployment runs officially at around 3.5 per cent – which is, however, considered a major understatement. Underemployment is high, and roughly a quarter of the employed labour force is made up of unpaid family members in rural areas, with only 27 per cent waged employees. In the early 1980s, 10 per cent of the labour work force worked abroad, mainly in the Middle East, but many have since returned home.

Pakistan has gradually opened up its economy, with around a third of GDP coming from exports, of which raw cotton accounts for 13 per cent, cotton yarn and thread 12 per cent, cotton fabrics 10 per cent, rice 8 per cent, leather 6 per cent, carpets and rugs 6 per cent, fish and fish preparations 2 per cent and sports goods 1.5 per cent. Major trading partners are the USA, Japan, Germany, the UK, Hong Kong, Italy, the United Arab Emirates, Ghana and the Republic of Korea.

The country's main imports are machinery and transport equipment, mineral fuels and lubricants, manufactured goods, food and live animals. The main sources for these are the USA, Japan, Kuwait, Germany, the UK, Saudi Arabia, China, Malaysia, the Republic of Korea and France. In terms of economic categories, 36 per cent consists of capital goods, 49 per cent of industrial raw materials and 15 per cent of consumer goods.

Cotton is the country's main cash crop and the largest foreign exchange earner, with productivity rising as greater use is made of insecticides. Rice is also an important export. Pakistan has a cropped area of around 20.8 million hectares. About one fifth of this is cultivated arable. River and ground water is plentiful, and the country's network of irrigation canals has been another essential element in productivity. The main food crops grown include wheat, rice, maize, barley, millet, sorghum, sugar cane, ground nuts, pulses, rapeseed, sesame, potatoes, onions, mangoes and citrus fruit. Livestock and the raising of goats, sheep, cattle, buffaloes, pigs, donkeys, horses, mules, camels and poultry accounts for nearly 8 per cent of the GDP, providing meat, eggs, dairy products, leather and wool, as well as draught power and fertiliser for cultivation. Seven per cent of the total land area is in pasture, while forests cover 4 per cent but contribute little to the economy. Most logging is for fuel wood. For the encouragement of agriculture, incentives such as price support, supply of basic materials at subsidised rates and provision of credit have given the sector a boost.

Manufactured goods account for 72 per cent of Pakistan's exports and just over 16.5 per cent of the GDP. There is a growing reliance on the new maharajahs in the private sector, with 85 per cent of manufacturing taking place in their factories. Refinery products include lubricating oil, naphtha, kerosene, diesel oil and furnace oil, with petrochemical capacity for benzene, toluene and xylene. The textile industry is the leading sector, although cotton cloth production has been declining in recent years, while cotton yarn increases. Other main industries are sugar refining, chemicals, food processing, sports goods, surgical instruments and paper. Construction accounts for just under 5 per cent of the GDP. Tourism has been slow to develop, due to continuing problems with India (Kashmir would be a prime tourist spot otherwise) and a lack of facilities.

Mining accounts for just under 1 per cent of the GDP, and about 67 per cent of the mining output comes from coal, crude oil and natural gas. There are estimated coal reserves of 580 million tonnes, while reserves of natural gas are thought to be around 441.13 billion cubic metres. Limestone, rock salt, gypsum, silica sand, china clay and chromite deposits are mined, and there are development plans for phosphate from Kakul and gold, silver and copper from Saindak in Baluchistan. Other minerals include iron ore, gem stones, magnetite, barites, antimony, bauxite, celestite, dolomite, fireclay, fluorite, fuller's earth, marble and soapstone. Exploration and extraction, however, are frequently hampered by difficult terrain.

Pakistan meets about 30 per cent of its current energy needs through imports. Domestic oil consumption is still growing fast, but the proven reserves of oil and coal will be sufficient to meet the country's requirements for the next thirty years. Like India, Pakistan also has access to nuclear power.

## Cities
The main cities are: Islamabad (population 515,000); Karachi (5,208,000); Lahore (2,953,000); Faisalabad (1,104,000) Rawalpindi (795,000); Hyderabad (751,000).

## Language
The official language is Urdu, but English is quite widely spoken in business circles.

## Media
Pakistan has 105 Urdu daily newspapers, published on a semi-national basis, and 14 English-language papers, including the *Pakistan Times*. There are 16 radio stations, and the national service broadcasts in numerous languages on several channels, with an external service in 15 different languages. There are also 5 TV stations, broadcasting for at least 10 hours a day.

## Climate

The country's terrain ranges from mountainous to desert, and the climate varies accordingly. It is cool in the mountains and foothills, with rain in summer and snow in winter, while in plateau regions it is hot in summer and cool in winter. The Indus Valley experiences year-round heat, with dry winds in the summer. Temperatures also vary, from an average 15°C in January to 37°C during May to July. Summer temperatures can rise as high as 50°C in northern Sind and eastern Baluchistan. The monsoon season lasts from mid July to September, when the average monthly rainfall drops to 16 cm. The best time for business travel is probably between October and April.

## Entry Requirements

Visas are required by most visitors: check with the embassy nearest to you. Foreigners require permits for visits to restricted zones in Kashmir. Such travel is distinctly inadvisable during the present troubles. Personal effects are allowed duty-free. Visitors are not permitted to import alcoholic beverages in any quantity.

## Health Requirements

Vaccination certificates are required for cholera and yellow fever when travelling from an infected area.

## Transport

The International airports are: Quaïd-e-Azam International (KHI), 12 km north-east of Karachi; Lahore (LHE), 11 km south-east of the city; Peshawar (PEW), 4 km from Peshawar; and Islamabad International Airport (ISB), 8 km from the city.

Roads run from Afghanistan via Qandhar–Chaman–Quetta or Kabul–Peshawar; from India via Amritsar–Lahore; and from China: the 805-km Karakoram Highway, serving Sinkian Province, Islamabad and Rawalpindi, via the Khunjerab Pass.

## Hotels

KARACHI
Beach Hotel, Moulvi Tamizuddin Khan Road, New Queen's Rd. Tel: 551031-7
Faran, Pechs, Shahra-E-Falosal Nursery. Tel: 430201
Holiday Inn Karachi, 9 Abdullah Haroon Road. Tel: 520111 Fax: 511610

Jabees, Abdullah Haroon Road, 0301. Tel: 512011–5
Karachi Airport Hotel, 11 Stargate Road. Tel: 480141–5
Mehran, Shah–reh–E–Faisal. Tel: 515061
Metropole, Club Road. Tel: 512051 Fax: 514301
Midway House, Karachi Airport, Stargate Road. Tel: 460371–5
Plaza International, 18-2 Civil Libes, Dr. David Pota Road. Tel: 520351
Ramada Renaissane, Avari Towers, Fatima Jinnah Road. Tel: 525261 Fax: 510310
Sheraton, Club Road. Tel: 521021 Fax: 512875
Taj Mahal Hotel, Shahrah–e–Faisal 0408. Tel: 520211
United Hotel, David Pota Road, Saddar. Tel: 515010–4
LAHORE
Faletti's, Egerton Road, PO Box 144. Tel: 303660
Hilton International Lahore, 87 Sharah–e–Quaid–e–Azam. Tel: 69971
International Hotel, Shahrah–e–Quaid–e–Azam. Tel: 870281
Pearl Continental Hotel, Shahrah–e–Quaid–e–Azam. Tel: 69931, 67931 Fax: 58760
PESHAWAR
Dean's, Islamia Road, Tel: 79781–3
Pearl Continental, Khyber Road, PO Box 197. Tel: 78361 Fax: 76285
RAWALPINDI
Flashman's, 17-22 The Mall, Tel: 581480–4
Pearl Continental, The Mall, PO Box 211 Tel: 66011
Shalimar Hotel, off The Mall, PO Box 93 Tel: 62901–9

## Credit Cards

There are now many places in Pakistan which accept Mastercard, Visa, Diner's and American Express.

## Working Hours

Business and government hours:
0900–1300 Saturday – Wednesday
0900–1100 Thursday
Banking hours: Sun–Thurs 0900–1330; Sat 0900–1100
Shops: Sat–Thurs 0800 or 0900 to 1800 or 1900

## Social Customs

The country follows an Islamic code of behaviour with sometimes strict consequences for offenders against the religious laws. This is also applied to banking and other areas of business. Ten years ago the country adopted Islamic banking practices which do not allow a saver to accrue interest as this is generally understood in most countries. Instead 'profit-and-loss' accounts divide net profit or loss of a bank between all depositors in ratio to money held. In some areas of Pakistan, for example the north in the Hunza and the Chitral Valleys, it is important that no photographs are taken of any military bases, bridges or airports. As a general principle, it is also unwise anywhere at any time to photograph any women without their express permission.

## Public Holidays
23 March (Pakistan Day)
1 May
14 August (Independence Day)
6 September
11 September
9 November
25 December (Founders Day)

## Telephone
Dialling code for Pakistan: IDD access code (00 from the UK), followed by 92, followed by area code:
Islamabad **51**
Karachi **21**
Lahore **42**
Rawalpindi **51**
(NB: Time zone is GMT + 5 hours)

## Electricity Supply
The current runs at 220–240 volts.

## Weights and Measures
Metric system.

## Banking
In July 1985 Pakistan adopted Islamic banking practices, which forbid payment of interest. The profit and loss accounts of a bank instead divide the net profit or loss among its depositors in propor-

tion to their savings. The country's main banking centre is Karachi, and the central bank is the State Bank of Pakistan.

## International Organisations
Pakistan is a member of the following:

Asian Development Bank
Colombo Plan
The Commonwealth
Economic Cooperation Organisation
The EC Trade and Cooperation Agreement
ESCAP
FAO
G77
General Agreement on Tariffs & Trade
ICAC
ICC
IFAD
IHO
IMO
INTELSAT
International Atomic Energy Agency
International Bank for Reconstruction & Development (UN)
International Civil Aviation Organisation (UN)
International Development Association (UN)
International Finance Corporation (UN)
International Labour Organisation
International Monetary Fund
Interpol
IPU
IRC
Islamic Conference Organisation
Islamic Development Bank
ITU
IWC
NAM
OIC
South Asian Association for Regional Cooperation
United Nations
United Nations Educational, Scientific and Cultural Organisation

United Nations Industrial Development Organisation
Universal Postal Union
WFFU
World Bank
World Health Organisation
World Intellectual Property Organisation
World Meteorological Organisation
WSG
World Trade Organisation

## (III) GUIDE TO BANGLADESH

In the days of a united British India, the country that is now Bangladesh occupied the extreme eastern part of the country. Upon Independence in 1947 that same area became East Pakistan. It had a majority of the population of all Pakistan, but much the smaller land area and always less political, military and economic clout. The feeling of neglect by rulers more than a thousand miles away in Karachi and Rawalpindi led to growing tensions between the two parts of Pakistan. General elections in 1970 gave the eastern-based Awami League an absolute majority in the National Assembly and committed it to a programme of autonomy. But the military rulers and parties in West Pakistan did not like this, and after unsuccessful negotiations the Awami League leader was arrested and a crackdown began. Guerrilla struggles followed until, on 16 December 1971, the freedom fighters, backed by the Indian Army, entered Dhaka and a secular socialist democratic republic of Bangladesh was declared.

The new country has had an unsettled history. Its first leader, Sheikh Mujibur Rahman, was assassinated in August 1975. General Ziaur Rahman, a Pakistan army major turned freedom fighter, took over, but in 1981 was himself assassinated after rivalry among senior military officers. After a bloodless coup in 1982, General Hussain Mohamed Ershad seized power and remained president for eight years until December 1990, when he was forced to step down after a concerted six-week campaign to oust him.

With Ershad safely off the throne, the unity of the opposition broke up, and in the elections that followed, 79 political parties, and 2,782 candidates, contested the country's 300 parliamentary seats. The two major parties were both led by women, each of whom was the closest surviving relative of an assassinated former leader. Begum

Khaleda Zia, the widow of Ziaur Rahman and leader of the Bangladesh National Party (BNP), proved the stronger of the two, with the Awami League, led by Sheikh Hasina Wazed, the daughter of Sheikh Mujibur Rahman, in second place. Begum Khaleda Zia's victory was a surprise to many people, for not only did she lack political experience, but her party, a recent creation, lacked the well-attested grass-roots support enjoyed by the Awami League.

In March 1994 the BNP was surprisingly defeated in the Dhaka municipal elections. After the opposition began agitating for fresh elections, there was an outright boycott of parliament, followed by the *en masse* resignation of the opposition. Recent elections confirmed the Begum's hold on power.

Bangladesh's 115 million people have to suffer a very frugal existence, with a per capital income assessed by the World Bank at $170 a year. The country is bigger in population terms than the world's other six poorest nations put together, and is also far smaller in terms of land area than any of the other eight poorest countries, with the exception of Malawi. Bangladesh's 144,000 square km of land, however, does include the mighty river waters of the Ganga-Brahmaputra system, the world's biggest river delta. When times are good, the river's waters, refreshed by the melting snows from the Himalayas, help to produce good soil and good crops.

The last two decades, however, have been a time of bad weather, worsening terms of trade, cuts in aid and population rises of about 2.3 per cent a year, meaning that any small gains in income were eaten up by a larger number of mouths. The IMF judged the country's economy to be 'beset with severe structural weaknesses including a narrow export base, a low domestic savings rate, and an under-developed financial sector'. Nevertheless, there were some real achievements. In 1990 the food grain harvest reached almost 20 million tonnes, not only a record but also close to self-sufficiency. Besides the traditional rice crop, Bangladesh has successfully cultivated wheat, which is far less reliant than rice on extensive irrigation. The total wheat crop is more than 2 million tonnes. The textile industry is booming too, and there is also progress in the electronics industry.

## Political parties

The main parties in Bangladesh are still the Bangladesh National Party (BNP), the Awami League, the Jatiya (People's) Party and the right-wing Jamaat-Islami. The country has a vast number of other parties as well.

## Population

Bangladesh's population has one of the highest densities in the world, at around 760 per square kilometre. Growth is now averaging 2.6 per cent per annum. According to a recent census, 47 per cent of this population are under fourteen. Some 85 per cent of people live in rural areas. Islam was decreed to be the state religion in 1988, and Muslims make up 86 per cent of the country's people. However, there are also approximately 650,000 Christians and Buddhists.

## Business Sectors

Agriculture employs 85 per cent of the workforce, accounts for a declining 47 per cent of the GDP and provides the bulk of exports. The land is very fertile, but productivity is hampered by fragmentation of holdings, reliance on traditional crops, drought and floods. The vast majority of the available land is farmed at a subsistence level.

Bangladesh relies heavily on foreign aid to keep the economy going. An annual injection of over $2 billion provides 40 per cent of government revenues, 50 per cent of foreign exchange and 90 per cent of the budget. Another important contribution is remittances from Bangladeshis working abroad, which have at times been higher than earnings from jute, the country's main export. Because the economy is mainly agricultural, it remains vulnerable to changes in weather and world commodity markets. In 1987 severe drought was followed by some of the worst flooding of the century. Only a year later, even worse floods inundated three-quarters of the land area. Another drought followed in 1989. Civil strife, lack of capital, reliance on jute exports and rapid population growth have also hampered economic development over the years. Recently the government has tried to open up the economy by emphasising private enterprise, encouraging foreign investment and setting up an export processing zone at Chittagong. Two further zones, at Khulna and Dhaka, are in an advanced planning stage. The last two years have seen a successful start to industrial exports, and an increasing number of joint ventures with foreign companies have been sanctioned.

Bangladesh's main exports are jute manufactures and raw jute (together accounting for 30 per cent of all exports), garments, fish, leather and tea. In the late 1980s the country also began assembling electronic goods for export. The main destinations for exported goods are the USA, Italy, the UK, Singapore, Germany, Japan, the CIS, Russia, Belgium, China, Iran and Pakistan. The country's main imports are manufactured goods, machinery and transport equipment, petroleum and petroleum products, chemicals and pharmaceuticals, vegetable oil and fats, inedible crude materials and food grains.

The industrial sector accounts for just over 10 per cent of the workforce, and the main activities are in jute, spinning and weaving. Textiles and industries are the fastest growth area. Other products include cigarettes, paper, flour, edible oils, skins and hides, tea and machinery. Bangladesh is self-sufficient in gas, with proven reserves estimated to be sufficient for the next ninety years. Demand for gas has doubled, so there are plans afoot to develop further fields.

## Cities
The main cities are; Dhaka (population 5 million); Chittagong (1.67 million); Chalna; Khulna; Narayanganj; Comilla; Rajshahi; Bogra.

## Language
The official language is Bengali, known locally as Bangla, which is spoken by 99 per cent of the population. However, English is also used, especially in business circles.

## Publications
There are 83 national daily newspapers (nine of them in English) and 43 other daily periodicals. *Ittefaq* is the most popular Bengali daily. There are also some 264 weekly newspapers, and 35 fortnightly and 117 monthly publications. There are few trade publications.

## Broadcasting
National broadcasting services maintain eight radio channels, with regional coverage in several languages. Government services broadcast one TV channel in Dhaka, Chittagong, Sylhet, Khulna, Natore, Mymensing and Rangpu.

## Climate
The climate is hot and humid, with an annual average rainfall of 2,500 mm, which mostly falls from April to October. The monsoon rains fall between June and September. The mean temperature in

April is around 38°C, and in November to March between 21 and 27°C during the day but as low as 10°C by night.

## Entry Requirements

Passports are required by all visitors, and visas by everyone except for nationals from Bhutan, Barbados, Cyprus, Fiji, New Zealand, Western Samoa, Nigeria, Kenya, Somalia, Nauru, Bahamas, Grenada, Papua New Guinea, Seychelles, Trinidad & Tobago, Guyana, Sri Lanka (for a stay not exceeding one month), Ireland, Tunisia, Vatican, Gabon, Spain, Mauritius, Malaysia, Malawi, The Gambia, Swaziland, Botswana, Jamaica, Guyana and Sierra Leone. Nationals of Yugoslavia, Japan and the Republic of Korea do not need a visa if they are in the country for less than three months. All those intending to work must have a suitable visa.

Personal effects are allowed entry duty-free provided they are declared on entry. No export licences are required for gifts or souvenirs whose total value is less than Tk3,000 (approximately $70). There are strict licensing requirements for all imports and restrictions on the importation of luxury goods.

## Currency

Foreign exchange may be brought into the country, providing a written declaration is made at the time of entry. No declaration is needed for amounts under $150.

## Health Requirements

Vaccination certificates are required for typhoid and cholera, and for yellow fever if travelling from an infected area. Regulations regarding travellers' health change frequently, so make detailed enquiries well in advance of travelling.

## Transport

Bangladesh's national airline is Biman Bangladesh Airlines. An airport tax of Tk250 is payable upon departure. The international airports are the Zia International (DAC), which is 20 km north of Dhaka; and Patenga (CGP), 22 km from Chittagong. There are regional airports at Jessore, Ishurdi, Saidpur, Syihet, Cox's Bazar, Comilla and Thakurgaon.

It is possible to get into Bangladesh from a number of different areas in India, including West Bengal, Assam and Tripura, but access is difficult during the monsoon. Over half the country's 9,300-km road network outside municipal areas is of good quality, with a metal surface. Limousine transfer is available between the airports and city hotels. Car rental is also an option but is probably not advisable except for the hardiest of travellers. Driving is on the left-hand side of the road. In the cities, taxis are available at main hotels and airports. It is essential to bargain a fare before setting out on a journey, and a tip of 10 per cent is expected. With rickshaws, too, negotiation of fares is advisable.

The railway network covers some 2,750 km and serves big cities. As elsewhere on the subcontinent, trains can be slow and subject to major delays. The main rail routes are Dhaka–Chittagong (journey time five hours) and Khulna–Ishurdi–Chilhati (journey time ten hours).

The country's main sea ports are Chittagong and Chalna. There are 7,000 km of navigable waterways, with regular passenger steamer services to the five main ports of Dhaka, Narayanganj, Chandpur, Barisal and Khulna. Tickets should be booked well in advance. There are six classes of graded travel, but only air-conditioned travel in first class is worthy of recommendation.

## Hotels

Accounts must be settled by credit card, traveller's cheques or hard currency. Major credit cards such as American Express, Mastercard and Visa are accepted in all major hotels and travel agencies. Towns in the provinces often have government rest houses which may be booked in advance.

The main hotels are:

### The Agrabad
Agrabad Commercial Area
PO Box 147
Chittagong
Tel: 500111/20

### The Shaikat
Station Road
Chittagong
Tel: 220181/2

## The Abakash
83–88 Mahakhaii C/A
Dhaka
Tel: 607085/9

## The Dhaka Sheraton
1 Minto Road 1000
PO Box 504
Tel: 505061
Fax: 412972

## The Purbani International
1 Dilkosha Commercial Area
Motijheel 2
Dhaka
Tel: 254081/6

## The Sonargon
Kaman Bazar
PO Box 3595
Dhaka
Tel: 315001
Fax: 411324

## Public Holidays
1 January (Bank Holiday)
21 February (Martyrs' Day)
26 March (Independence and National Day)
15 April (Bengali New Year)
1 May (May Day)
1 July (Bank Holiday)
23 October (Durga Puja)
7 November (National Revolution Day)
16 December (Victory Day)
25 December (Christmas Day)
   There are also a number of holidays that vary according to the
Muslim Calendar. These are: Good Friday and Easter Monday,
Shab-e-Barat, Shab-e-Qadr, Eid-al-Fitr, Eid-al-Adha, the Prophet's
Birthday, Jam at-ul-Wida, Budha Purnima, Durga Puja (Dashami),
Muharram, Eid-e-Miladunnabi.

149

## Working Hours

For the government and business in general, hours are 9 a.m. to 4 p.m. Saturday to Thursday, with offices closed on Friday. Lunch hour is taken between 12.30 and 1.30. Banking hours are 9 a.m. to 1 p.m. Saturday to Wednesday, and 9 a.m. to 11 a.m. on Thursdays.

## Social Customs

Drinking, smoking and eating in public causes the worst possible offence during Ramadan. Under no circumstances should photographs be taken of women.

## Telephone

Telecommunications are still primitive and faxes are rare. Where they exist the lines are often down anyway. Patience and persistence are essential.

Dialling code for Bangladesh: IDD access code (00 from the UK), followed by 880, followed by area code:

Dhaka **2**
Chittagong **31**
(NB: Time zone is GMT + 6 hours)

## Electricity Supply

The supply is 220–240 volts AC, with a British-type 2- or 3-pin round plug.

## Banking

The country's banking centre is in Dhaka, and the central bank is the Bangladesh Bank.

Bangladesh Bank
Motijheel C/A
PO Box 325
Dhaka 1000
Tel: 235000/09

Agrani Bank
9D Dilkusha C/A Motijheel
PO Box 531
Dhaka 1000
Tel: 322982/7

Bangladesh Khrisi Bank
83–85 Motijheel C/A
Dhaka 1000
Tel: 240021/5

Janata Bank
110 Motijheel C/A
PO Box 468
Dhaka 1000
Tel: 236242/9

Rupali Bank Ltd
Rupali Bhaban 34
Dilkusha C/A
PO Box 719
Dhaka 1000
Tel: 251827

Sonali Bank
Motijheel C/A
PO Box 147
Dhaka 1000
Tel: 252990/8

**Other Useful Addresses**
Tourism and business Travel Information:

Bangladesh Parjatan Corporation
Airport Road
Trejgaon
Dhaka 12
Tel: 325155/9

Bangladesh Jute Mills Corp.
Adamjee Court
4th Floor Motijheel Commercial Area
Dhaka
Tel: 238182

The Export Promotions Bureau
122 Motijheel Commercial Area
Dhaka
Tel: 232245/9

**International Organisations**
Bangladesh is a member of the following:
Afro-Asian People's Solidarity Organisation
Asian Development Bank
CCC
Colombo Plan
The Commonwealth
EC Trade and Cooperation Agreement
ESCAP
FAO
General Agreement of Tariffs & Trade
G77
IFAD
International Civil Aviation Organisation (UN)
International Development Association (UN)
International Finance Corporation (UN)
International Labour Organisation (UN)
Interpol
IOC
IRC
Islamic Conference Organisation
Islamic Development Bank
ITU
NAM
OIC
South Asian Association for Regional Cooperation
UNCTAD
United Nations
Universal Postal Union
World Health Organisation
World Intellectual Property Organisation
World Meteorological Organisation

# Appendix 2:

# Major Players

# The Birla Group

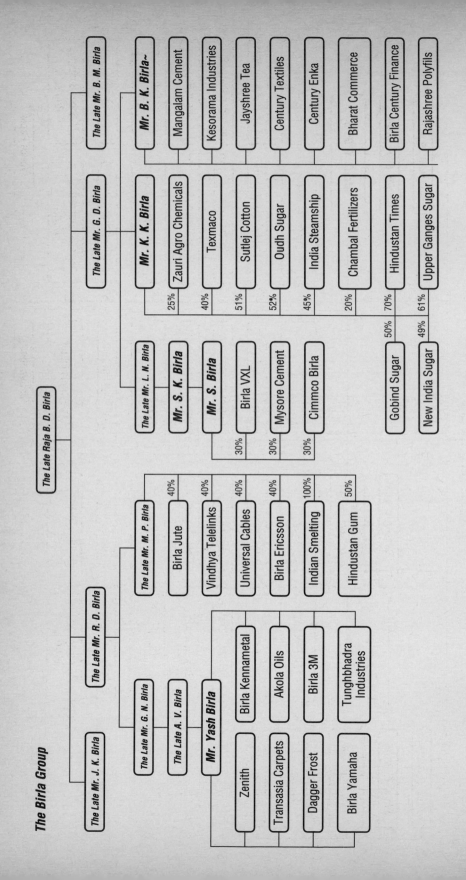

The Late Raja B. D. Birla

**The Late Mr. J. K. Birla** | **The Late Mr. R. D. Birla** | **The Late Mr. G. D. Birla** | **The Late Mr. B. M. Birla**

The Late Mr. G. N. Birla
The Late Mr. A. V. Birla
**Mr. Yash Birla**

The Late Mr. M. P. Birla

The Late Mr. L. N. Birla
**Mr. K. K. Birla**
**Mr. B. K. Birla~**

**Mr. S. K. Birla**
**Mr. S. Birla**

## Mr. Yash Birla
- Zenith
- Birla Kennametal
- Transasia Carpets
- Akola Oils
- Dagger Frost
- Birla 3M
- Birla Yamaha
- Tunghbhadra Industries

## The Late Mr. M. P. Birla
- Birla Jute — 40%
- Vindhya Telelinks
- Universal Cables — 40%
- Birla Ericsson — 40%
- Indian Smelting — 100%
- Hindustan Gum — 50%

## Mr. S. Birla
- Birla VXL — 30%
- Mysore Cement — 30%
- Cimmco Birla — 30%

## Mr. K. K. Birla
- Zuari Agro Chemicals — 25%
- Texmaco — 40%
- Sutlej Cotton — 51%
- Oudh Sugar — 52%
- India Steamship — 45%
- Chambal Fertilizers — 20%
- Hindustan Times — 70%
- Upper Ganges Sugar — 61%
- Gobind Sugar — 50%
- New India Sugar — 49%

## Mr. B. K. Birla~
- Mangalam Cement
- Kesorama Industries
- Jayshree Tea
- Century Textiles
- Century Enka
- Bharat Commerce
- Birla Century Finance
- Rajashree Polyfils

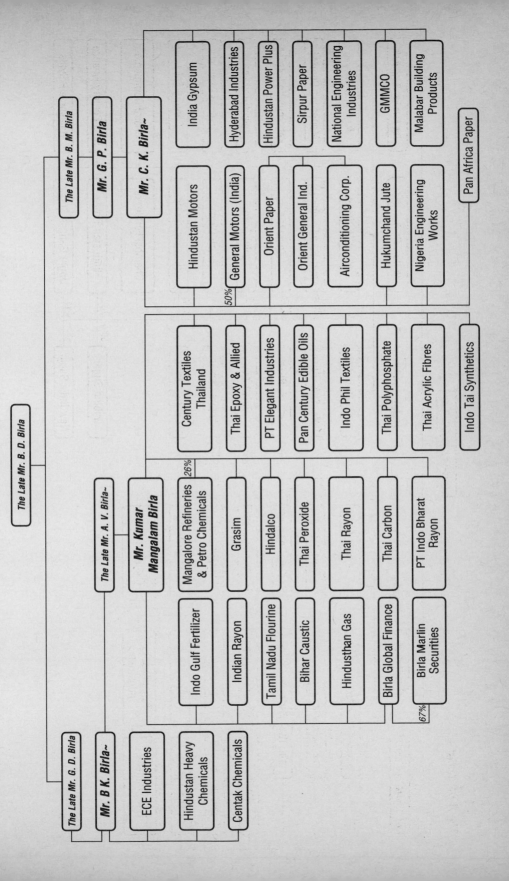

The Late Mr. B. D. Birla

**The Late Mr. G. D. Birla**

**Mr. B K. Birla~**

ECE Industries

Hindustan Heavy Chemicals

Centak Chemicals

**The Late Mr. A. V. Birla~**

**Mr. Kumar Mangalam Birla**

Indo Gulf Fertilizer

Mangalore Refineries & Petro Chemicals — 26%

Indian Rayon

Grasim

Tamil Nadu Flourine

Hindalco

Bihar Caustic

Thai Peroxide

Hindusthan Gas

Thai Rayon

Birla Global Finance

Thai Carbon

Birla Marlin Securities — 67%

PT Indo Bharat Rayon

Century Textiles Thailand

Thai Epoxy & Allied

PT Elegant Industries

Pan Century Edible Oils

Indo Phil Textiles

Thai Polyphosphate

Thai Acrylic Fibres

Indo Tai Synthetics

**The Late Mr. B. M. Birla**

**Mr. G. P. Birla**

**Mr. C. K. Birla~**

India Gypsum

Hindustan Motors

General Motors (India) — 50%

Hyderabad Industries

Hindustan Power Plus

Orient Paper

Orient General Ind.

Sirpur Paper

Airconditioning Corp.

National Engineering Industries

Hukumchand Jute

GMMCO

Nigeria Engineering Works

Malabar Building Products

Pan Africa Paper

## The Hinduja Group

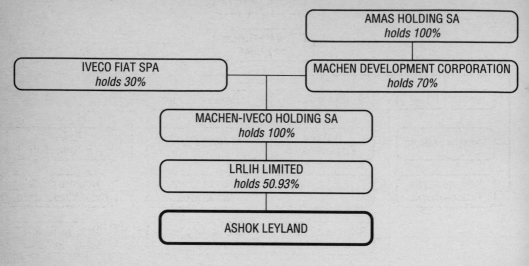

## The Reliance Group

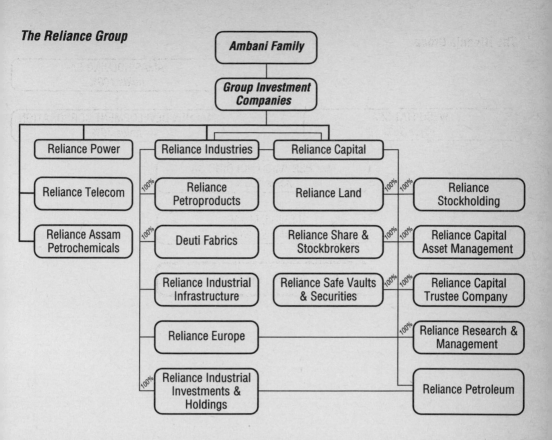

# The Tata Group

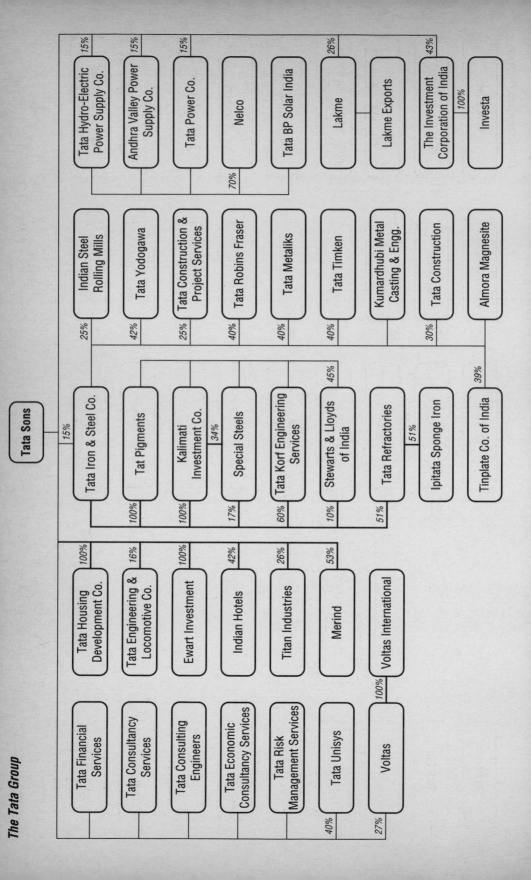

**Tata Sons** — 15%

## Tata Iron & Steel Co.
- Indian Steel Rolling Mills — 25%
- Tata Yodogawa — 42%
- Tata Construction & Project Services — 25%
- Tata Robins Fraser — 40%
- Tata Metaliks — 40%
- Tata Timken — 40%
- Kumardhubi Metal Casting & Engg. — 30%
- Tata Construction
- Almora Magnesite

- Tat Pigments — 100%
- Kalimati Investment Co. — 100%
- Special Steels — 34% / 17%
- Tata Korf Engineering Services — 60%
- Stewarts & Lloyds of India — 45% / 10%
- Tata Refractories — 51%
- Ipitata Sponge Iron — 51%
- Tinplate Co. of India — 39%

- Tata Hydro-Electric Power Supply Co. — 15%
- Andhra Valley Power Supply Co. — 15%
- Tata Power Co. — 15%
- Nelco — 70%
- Tata BP Solar India
- Lakme — 26%
- Lakme Exports
- The Investment Corporation of India — 43%
- Investa — 100%

- Tata Financial Services
- Tata Consultancy Services
- Tata Consulting Engineers
- Tata Economic Consultancy Services
- Tata Risk Management Services
- Tata Unisys
- Voltas — 27%
- Voltas International — 100%

- Tata Housing Development Co. — 100%
- Tata Engineering & Locomotive Co. — 16%
- Ewart Investment — 100%
- Indian Hotels — 42%
- Titan Industries — 26%
- Merind — 53%
- Voltas — 40%

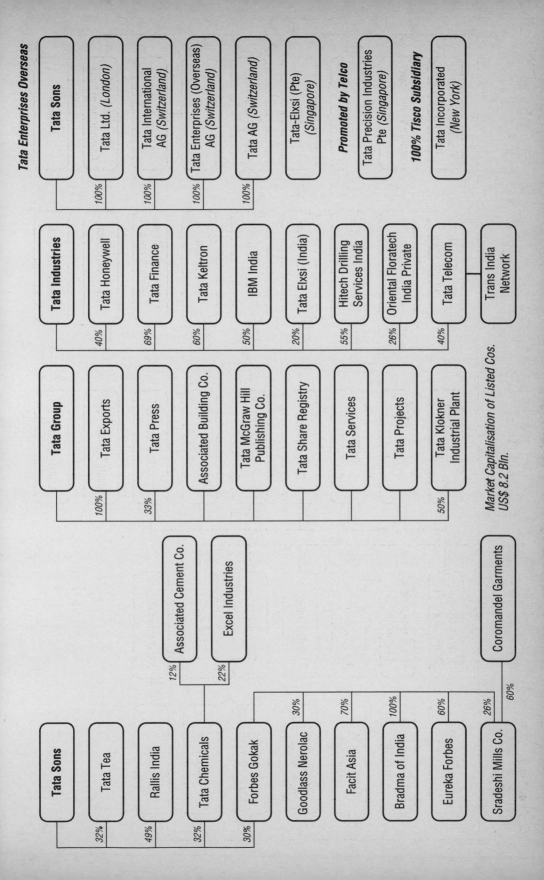

**Tata Enterprises Overseas**

**Tata Sons**
- Tata Ltd. *(London)* — 100%
- Tata International AG *(Switzerland)* — 100%
- Tata Enterprises (Overseas) AG *(Switzerland)* — 100%
- Tata AG *(Switzerland)* — 100%
- Tata-Elxsi (Pte) *(Singapore)*

**Promoted by Telco**
- Tata Precision Industries Pte *(Singapore)*

**100% Tisco Subsidiary**
- Tata Incorporated *(New York)*

**Tata Industries**
- Tata Honeywell — 40%
- Tata Finance — 69%
- Tata Keltron — 60%
- IBM India — 50%
- Tata Elxsi (India) — 20%
- Hitech Drilling Services India — 55%
- Oriental Floratech India Private — 26%
- Tata Telecom — 40%
  - Trans India Network

**Tata Group**
- Tata Exports — 100%
- Tata Press — 33%
- Associated Building Co.
- Tata McGraw Hill Publishing Co.
- Tata Share Registry
- Tata Services
- Tata Projects
- Tata Klokner Industrial Plant — 50%

*Market Capitalisation of Listed Cos.*
*US$ 8.2 Bln.*

**Tata Sons**
- Tata Tea — 32%
- Rallis India — 49%
- Tata Chemicals — 32%
- Forbes Gokak — 30%
  - Associated Cement Co. — 12%
  - Excel Industries — 22%
  - Goodlass Nerolac — 30%
  - Facit Asia — 70%
  - Bradma of India — 100%
  - Eureka Forbes — 60%
  - Sradeshi Mills Co. — 26%
    - Coromandel Garments — 60%

# Appendix 3:

# Vital Statistics – India

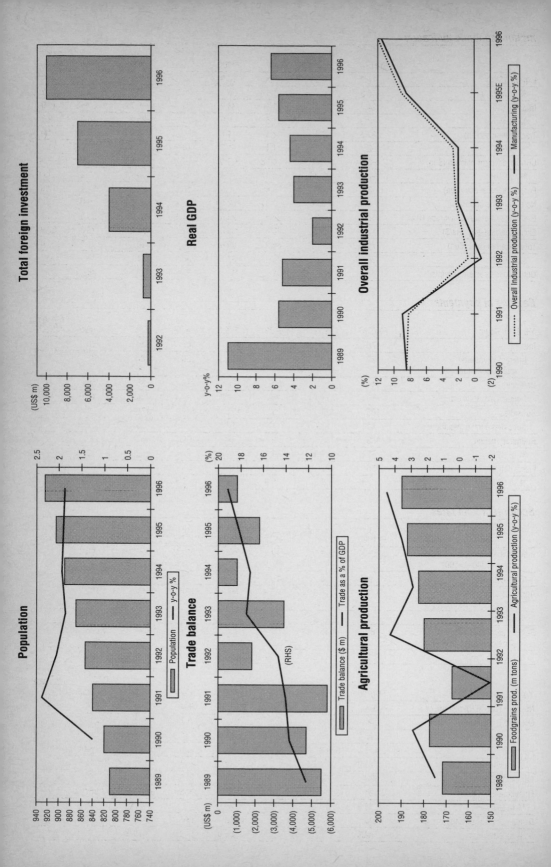

## Indian Economic Indicators

| | FY1990 | FY91 | FY92 | FY93 | FY94 | FY95 | FY96 | forecast FY1997 |
|---|---|---|---|---|---|---|---|---|
| Exports ($bn) | 17.0 | 18.5 | 18.3 | 18.9 | 22.7 | 26.8 | 31.3 | 36.0 |
| % growth | 18.9 | 9.0 | −1.1 | 3.3 | 20.3 | 17.9 | 16.8 | 15.2 |
| Imports ($bn) | 24.4 | 27.9 | 21.1 | 23.2 | 23.99 | 30.71 | 36.50 | 40.00 |
| % growth | 3.3 | 14.4 | −24.5 | 10.3 | 3.2 | 28.0 | 18.9 | 9.6 |
| Trade balance ($bn) | −7.5 | −9.4 | −2.8 | −4.4 | −1.3 | −3.9 | −5.3 | −4.0 |
| % to GDP | −2.7 | −3.2 | −1.1 | −1.8 | −0.5 | −1.3 | −1.6 | −1.1 |
| Current account balance ($bn) | −6.84 | −9.68 | −1.18 | −3.53 | −0.32 | −2.08 | −4.05 | −3.74 |
| % to GDP | −2.49 | −3.24 | −0.47 | −1.45 | −0.13 | −0.71 | −1.27 | −1.06 |
| Forex reserves–eoy ($bn) | 3.4 | 2.2 | 5.8 | 6.5 | 15.4 | 20.2 | 18.4 | 17.9 |
| No of months imports | 1.66 | 0.96 | 3.31 | 3.38 | 7.71 | 7.88 | 6.04 | 5.38 |
| Exchange rate-annual average (Rs/$) | 16.5 | 17.94 | 24.5 | 29.0 | 31.4 | 31.4 | 33.3 | 36.5 |
| Exchange rate–eoy (Rs/$) | 17.1 | 19.2 | 28.4 | 31.5 | 31.4 | 31.6 | 35.0 | 37.0 |
| Total external debt ($bn) | 75.9 | 84.0 | 85.3 | 90.0 | 90.7 | 90.5 | 101.0 | 105.0 |
| % of GDP | 28 | 28 | 34 | 37 | 36 | 31 | 32 | 30 |
| Debt service/current receipts | 43 | 45 | 41 | 41 | 35 | 39 | 38 | 39 |

## Balance of payments

| Y/e 31/3, Rs bn | FY1990 | FY91 | FY92 | FY93 | FY94 | FY95 | FY96 | forecast FY1997 |
|---|---|---|---|---|---|---|---|---|
| Interest | 178 | 215 | 266 | 311 | 367 | 440 | 520 | – |
| Interest payments/ total expenditure (%) | 19 | 20 | 24 | 25 | 26 | 27 | 30 | – |
| Defence | 144 | 154 | 163 | 176 | 218 | 235 | 255 | – |
| Defence exp/total exp (%) | 15.5 | 14.6 | 14.7 | 14.3 | 15.4 | 14.5 | 14.8 | – |
| Subsidies | 105 | 122 | 123 | 120 | 129 | 128 | 124 | – |
| Subsidies/total expenditure (%) | 11 | 12 | 11 | 10 | 9 | 8 | 7 | – |
| Budgetary deficit | −106 | −113 | −69 | −123 | −110 | −60 | −50 | – |
| % to GDP | −2.3 | −2.1 | −1.1 | −1.8 | −1.4 | −0.7 | −0.5 | – |
| Fiscal deficit | 356 | 446 | 363 | 402 | 603 | 610 | 700 | – |
| % to GDP | 7.8 | 8.3 | 5.9 | 5.7 | 7.7 | 6.6 | 6.6 | – |

## Sectoral growth rates

| | FY1990 | FY91 | FY92 | FY93 | FY94 | FY95 | FY96 | forecast FY1997 |
|---|---|---|---|---|---|---|---|---|
| Industrial production Index (1980–1=100) | 196.4 | 212.5 | 212.5 | 218.9 | 227.8 | 244.7 | 263.3 | – |
| % growth | 8.6 | 8.2 | 0.0 | 3.0 | 4.1 | 7.4 | 7.6 | – |
| Agricultural production Index (1979–82=100) | 143.2 | 148.3 | 145.4 | 151.6 | 154.8 | 162.2 | 162.2 | – |
| % growth | 2.2 | 3.6 | −2.0 | 4.3 | 2.1 | 4.8 | 0.0 | – |
| Service sector income (Rs bn, 1980–1 prices) | 780 | 813 | 867 | 906 | 963 | 1,024 | 1,086 | – |
| % growth | 7.8 | 4.2 | 6.7 | 4.5 | 6.2 | 6.4 | 6.0 | – |

| Y/e 31/3, Rs bn | FY1990 | FY91 | FY92 | FY93 | FY94 | FY95 | FY96 | forecast FY1997 |
|---|---|---|---|---|---|---|---|---|
| Nominal GDP at market prices | 4,568 | 5,355 | 6,161 | 7,028 | 7,864 | 9,200 | 10,580 | – |
| Nominal GDP ($bn) | 274 | 299 | 252 | 242 | 251 | 293 | 320 | – |
| % growth | 15.4 | 17.2 | 15.0 | 14.1 | 11.9 | 17.0 | 15.0 | – |
| Per capita GDP (Rs) | 5,473 | 6,288 | 7,099 | 7,951 | 8,730 | 10,024 | 11,313 | – |
| % growth | 13.0 | 14.9 | 12.9 | 12.0 | 9.8 | 14.8 | 12.9 | – |
| Per capita GDP ($) | 329 | 350 | 290 | 274 | 278 | 319 | 342 | – |
| Final consumption | 3,424 | 3,922 | 4,510 | 4,980 | 5,655 | 6,667 | 7,667 | – |
| % to GDP | 75.0 | 73.2 | 73.2 | 70.9 | 71.9 | 72.5 | 72.5 | – |
| Gross domestic savings | 1,020 | 1,268 | 1,420 | 1,406 | 1,505 | 1,800 | 2,100 | – |
| % to GDP | 22.3 | 23.7 | 23.1 | 20.0 | 19.1 | 19.6 | 19.8 | – |

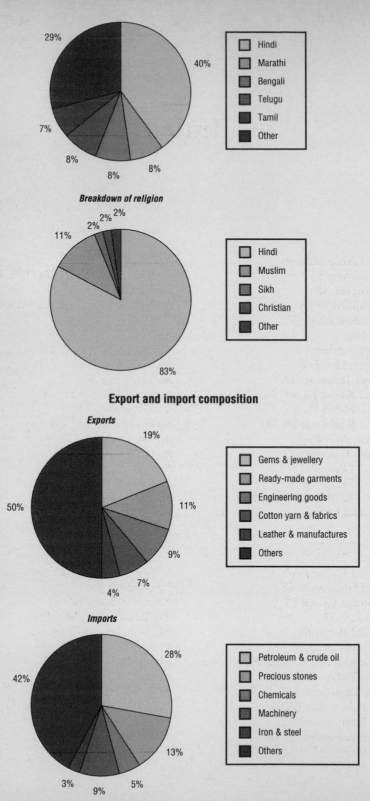

**Language spoken (% of population)**

- 40% Hindi
- 29% Other
- 7%
- 8%
- 8%
- 8%

Legend:
- Hindi
- Marathi
- Bengali
- Telugu
- Tamil
- Other

**Breakdown of religion**

- 83%
- 11%
- 2%
- 2%
- 2%

Legend:
- Hindi
- Muslim
- Sikh
- Christian
- Other

**Export and import composition**

*Exports*

- 19%
- 11%
- 9%
- 7%
- 4%
- 50%

Legend:
- Gems & jewellery
- Ready-made garments
- Engineering goods
- Cotton yarn & fabrics
- Leather & manufactures
- Others

*Imports*

- 28%
- 13%
- 5%
- 9%
- 3%
- 42%

Legend:
- Petroleum & crude oil
- Precious stones
- Chemicals
- Machinery
- Iron & steel
- Others

# Index

165